Microtonality in Ancient Greek Music

Dr Michael Hewitt

THE NOTE TREE
thenotetree.co.uk

Copyright © 2014 by Dr Mike Hewitt

Dr Michael Hewitt

All rights reserved. No part of this publication may be reproduced, distributed, or transmitted in any form or by any means, including photocopying, recording or other electronic or mechanical means, without the prior written permission of the publisher, except in the case of brief quotations embodied in critical views and certain other non-commercial uses permitted by copyright law.

First printing: 2014

ISBN:0957547013
ISBN-13:9780957547018

CONTENTS

0 Introduction — 1

1 Aristoxenus and the Commonwealth of Experience — Pg 4
The fine-tuning of musical scales... Origins of diatonic scales... Ancient Greek origins of diatonic scales... Schism between scale and tuning... The philosophy of Aristoxenus of Tarentum... A commonwealth of musical experience.

2 Pythagorean Arithmetic — Pg 18
Pythagorean number lore... Numbers of the decade... The Tetractys... Four stages of creation... The Tetractys and music... Pythagorean note ratios... Ratios as tools for acoustic investigation... The composition of ratios... Harmonic relationships... Ratios as designating note positions... Common operations... The monochord... Ancient Greek double octave.

3 Genesis of the Ancient Greek Scale System — Pg 37
Reconciling the viewpoints of Aristoxenus and Pythagoras... The four stringed lyre... The tuning of the lyre... The pentatonic tuning of the lyre... The heptachord of Terpander... Notes and planets... The Pythagorean octave scale... Relationships between the four fixed tones... The ancient Greek Dorian scale system... The correlation between notes and strings of the lyre.

4 The Greater Perfect System — Pg 54
The genera... Extension of the Dorian system... Tetrachords in Arabic maqamat... Ajnas... Modal tonic and dominant... The Arabic double octave... Root and branch tetrachords... Features of the

Greater Perfect System... The Lesser Perfect System... The Perfect or Immutable system.

5 The Seven Harmoniai — Pg 70

The modal tonic note... Modal functions... The mésē as modal tonic... The mésē as solar principle... The seven harmoniai... Eidos, or the seven octave species... Diatonic modes of Babylonian music... Ancient evidence for the seven modes ... The tuning up and down principle... The oldest song in the world... Pertinent questions... Planetary harmonies and the days of the week.

6 The Tonoi of Ptolemy — Pg 90

Mode and modulation... The seven tonoi... The thetic and dynamic mésē... The dynamic mésē as contributor to modal ethos...Characteristics of the seven modes... Pythagorean intonation.

7 The Shades — Pg 105

Chroai... Aristoxenus' diatonic modal shades... the intense diatonic shade... the soft diatonic shade.

8 Diatonic Shades of Ptolemy — Pg 117

A value for epimoric ratios... Ptolemy's ditonal diatonic shade... Ptolemy's intense diatonic shade... Didymus' diatonic tuning... Ptolemy's soft diatonic shade... Ptolemy's whole tone diatonic shade... Ptolemy's equable diatonic shade.

9 The Chromatic Genus — Pg 136

Constitution of the chromatic tetrachord... chromatic tetrachords in modern music... Pythagorean form of chromatic scale system ... pentatonic implications of the chromatic genus... chromatic octave species ... the seven chromatic modes.

10 Shades of the Chromatic Genus   Pg 149
Aristoxenus' intense chromatic shade... Aristoxenus' hemiolic chromatic shade... Aristoxenus' soft chromatic shade... Ptolemy's intense chromatic shade... Ptolemy's soft chromatic shade... alternative chromatic tunings.

11 The Enharmonic Genus   Pg 162
The enharmonic pyknon... the seven enharmonic modes... the enharmonic genus and major third pentatonic scales... the enharmonic scale of Olympus... the Spondeion mode... Ptolemy's enharmonic tuning.

12 Reviewing the Ancient Enharmonic System   Pg 173
The Pythagorean cyclic method of scale division... the pentatonic scale... the diatonic scale...the Pythagorean form of chromatic scale... the seeds of the enharmonic scale... the enharmonic scale of Safi al-Din... subtleties of intonation... the scale of enharmonic dieses.

Conclusion   Pg 203

Introduction

My last book *Musical Scales of the World*, looked at the various musical scales and modes that modern Western musicians might use today, including those advantageously borrowed or adapted from other non-Western cultures. In this book I intend to take the reader on a journey through much more ancient territory and by doing so, try to show that the musical scales and modes used by musicians today not only have their roots in an ancient past, but also, represent only a small fraction of the treasures of that ancient past.

As a musician, I find the study of the music of ancient cultures particularly fascinating. However, this study is not without its own peculiar difficulties. One of the most obvious difficulties that confronts the enquirer is that none of the original music has survived in a tangible form, bar in certain cases, the odd fragments of notated music, whose proper interpretation itself, is often fraught with problems. Perhaps this is the main obstacle that surrounds the study of the musical languages of ancient cultures. In contrast to the plastic arts, whose relatively durable materials often enable artistic works to outlive their creators, music is much more fleeting, its materials existing only in time.

Inevitably, any in-depth study of the music of the ancient world is a vast one, embracing as it does many ancient cultures. For this reason, I have always found it best to undertake this study by focusing upon one culture at a time. However, as ancient cultures often shared key ideas, concepts and approaches, it is probably wise to approach the study of the music or musical scales of a particular culture from a broad global standpoint, one that, on the one hand, recognizes the uniqueness of the music of that particular culture, yet on the other, recognizes that this music may share certain of its elements in common with other cultures. This volume shows a particular interest in the musical scales and modes of ancient Greece. However even here, this book will often refer to what might be called a shared heritage – certain features of music that cultures shared in common with one another.

In terms of the level and depth of approach to the subject, this is not intended to be an academic thesis on the subject. Neither is it intended to be a comprehensive study. It is primarily written for musicians who, like myself, find themselves fascinated with the subject of the music and musical scales of ancient cultures, and very much interested in exploring some of their facets.

For example, I love to tune my keyboard to some of the ancient Greek scales and then simply improvise, and by doing so immerse myself in the world of sound that each scale is uniquely capable of producing. This way, it is possible to discover for oneself that each scale seems to suggest certain moods and feelings, and that these are as marked in their own way, as those moods and feelings evoked for example by our bright major and darker minor scales.

Mood, colour and atmosphere – all features relating to that important quality of *ethos* as mentioned by ancient Greek philosophers and writers - can in this sense, be approached experientially, through the musician's direct involvement with the sound produced by a particular scale. This in its turn can significantly contribute to the musician's feeling for some of the moods that might have been evoked by this ancient and original music.

1 Aristoxenus and the Commonwealth of Experience

The major and minor scales with which Western musicians tend to be most familiar today, represent only a few out of what are probably thousands of possible scales, many of which are, or have been used by other cultures of the world. Accompanying this realization may come a feeling of surprise, especially since it is often assumed that, as the inevitable products of our musical evolution to date, these scales thereby represent the very best that is available, so far as musical scales are concerned.

The feeling of surprise is connected with the realization that this might not be the case, and that our common recognition of but a few scales, out of the thousands that are potentially available, represents a severe constraint upon the musician's artistic and musical freedom. At this point therefore, the musician may begin to undertake an investigation of the musical scales of other cultures, especially if there is seen to be some advantage to be gained by doing so. Principally, any advantage lies in the possibility for the expansion of the range of melodic and harmonic expression, by virtue of the use of such scales. As my last book showed, many such scales may be effectively utilized for this very purpose.

However, to use these scales it is often necessary to modify them in accordance with Western methods of tuning. This is because our principle musical instruments, among which are the guitar, piano, organ, etc., are all built in such a way as to constrain the user to operate within the limitations of a pre-set scale structure: the equally-tempered twelve-tone or chromatic scale.

Established well-over three hundred years ago, the equally tempered twelve-tone scale divides the octave space into twelve exactly equal semitones. This makes it very useful for specific musical purposes, namely those for which modulation to various keys is required. However, most of the musical scales of the world were never developed with equal temperament in mind. Because of this, their notes often fall between the 'cracks' of the keyboard so to speak. In effect therefore, the process of 'adapting' such scales will probably lead to a compromise of their original tuning.

In some notable cases this is not particularly significant. The major and minor third pentatonic scales of Japanese music for example, adapt quite well to an equally tempered format. This is because their original tuning, based on the cycle of fifths, does not depart too far from equally tempered norms. With other scales however, such as the Thai equatonal seven-toned scale, the process of adaption so disfigures the original scale, that it then becomes unrecognizable as such. Therefore, in this case, the process of adaption to a tempered format is not particularly productive.

The fine-tuning of musical scales...

In recent decades the situation has changed considerably through the development of electronic keyboards and their software equivalents, which often have fine-tuning options built into them. This fine-tuning process generally uses the system of cents, originally introduced by the English mathematician and theorist Alexander Ellis (1814 – 1890).

This system divides the equally tempered semitone into one hundred equal units, each unit being called a cent. As there are twelve such semitones per octave therefore, the octave space itself is equivalent to twelve-hundred cents. A diagrammatic representation of the system of cents can be seen in fig 1.1, in which the octave is portrayed as a circle whereby each semitone is represented as a one-twelfth segment of the octave circle. Each segment, as shown, is divisible into 100 further units.

Fig. 1.1: *Division of the Octave into Twelve Hundred Cents*

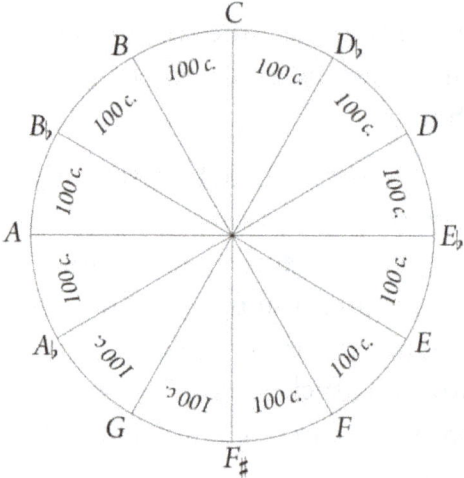

Given that the exact positions of the notes of a particular scale as measured in cents are known, this fine-tuning process thereby enables the user to tune their musical instrument specifically in order to be able to make use of that particular scale – without ever having to 'adapt' it to equal temperament. This definitely represents a move in the right direction, for rather than having to adapt the scale to suit the instrument, it is now the other way around. The instrument can be adapted to suit the scale – or at least it can, to a certain extent.

In terms of hardware, there are numerous makes of modern synthesizer workstations that allow one to tune any of the twelve notes of the scale to an increment of anything up to plus or minus 99 cents either way. This is a tremendous facility, for it means that many different world musical scales, including the scales of ancient Greece – whatever their particular type of tuning – can be accurately reproduced on a synthesizer workstation.

The tuning given in fig. 1.2 for example, is that required for the diatonic scale as proscribed by the fourth century BC Greek philosopher, mathematician and musical theorist Archytas of Tarentum (428 – 347 BC). Without the process of fine-tuning, Archytas diatonic scale would offer no more than a modern Western Phrygian mode. Through use of fine-tuning however, the scale can be used exactly as Archytas intended. In doing so, any difference with the equally tempered form will not only immediately be heard, but also a sense of literally being transported back into a vivid and colorful world of sound and tone that is over two-thousand years old will be experienced.

Fig. 1.2: Archytas' Diatonic Scale

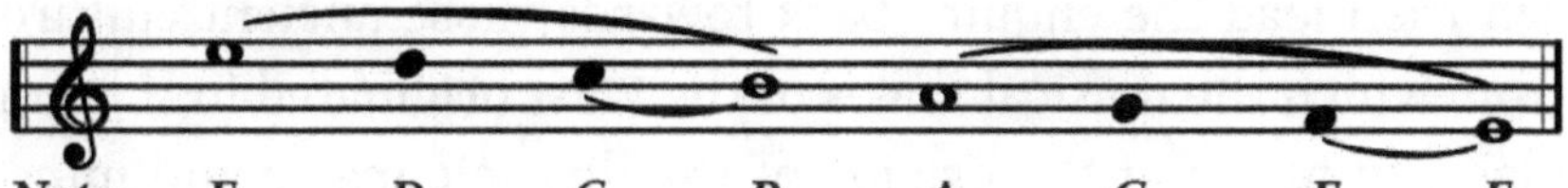

Note:	E	D	C	B	A	G	F	E
Cents:	1200	996	765	702	498	294	63	0

Looking at fig, 1.2 it becomes apparent that the notes are tuned very differently to their equally tempered counterparts, the latter always being tuned in round hundreds of cents. To fine tune an instrument to produce this scale:

- tune note F down by 37 cents;
- tune note G down by 6 cents;
- tune note A down by 2 cents;
- tune note C down by 35 cents;
- tune note D down by 4 cents;
- tune note B up by 2 cents.

By doing this the correct intonation with which to play Archytas ancient diatonic scale will be obtained.

Origins of diatonic scales...

Because of the fine-tuning options that are now so readily available, there is a growing interest amongst musicians, in musical scales and modes whose tuning is subtly different to modern Western equal temperament. This interest always tends to be further encouraged by an encounter with the world of modal colour thus made available, a world that may act as a direct spur to creativity, and a panacea against possible intellectual and artistic stagnation.

Naturally, this interest may be pursued in many different directions, one of which is the exploration of the history of the musical scales that are used in the West today. For this in itself can then lead the enquiry back towards those ancient cultures from which the musical scales of the West originated in the first place. In terms of the origins of the diatonic major and minor scales for example, the trace may begin with the role that the early Western church played in the process of the selection of those musical scales that were felt to be suitable for its purposes.

This process probably began around the fourth century under the influence of St Ambrose (340 – 397), the Bishop of Milan who sought a method for systematizing the extensive collection of sacred melodies that comprised the musical repertoire of the church at that time. The facility of scale and mode proved extremely useful for this process as the melodies could be categorized in terms of their mode.

The system Ambrose developed took the form of four basic diatonic modes. There was a mode on D that was termed *Protus* - the first mode, a mode on E termed *Deuterus* - the second mode, a mode on F termed *Tritus* - the third mode and finally, a mode on G termed *Tetrardus* - the fourth mode. See Table 1:

Table 1: *The Four Modes of Ambrose*

Protus:	D	E	F	G	A	B	C	D
Deuterus:	E	F	G	A	B	C	D	E
Tritus:	F	G	A	B	C	D	E	F
Tetrardus:	G	A	B	C	D	E	F	G

Under the influence of Pope Gregory (540-604), this basic system of four modes later underwent a process of expansion whereby it was developed into a system of eight modes, modelled upon the *octoechos* framework of the modes of Byzantine chant. In this new system the four original modes were termed authentic. Each authentic mode was then supplemented by a plagal mode, which although having the same final or tonic, nevertheless had a different melodic range or ambitus, which began a fourth below the corresponding plagal mode. Therefore the two forms of the first mode appear as follows. The tonic of both modes is shown in capitals:

Authentic Protus:	D	e	f	g	a	b	c	D
Plagal Protus:	a	b	c	D	e	f	g	a

The difference between the authentic and plagal modes was not just one of ambitus. The constitution of a mode was also determined by a two-note axis of *final* and *reciting tone*, the modal tonic and dominant tones respectively. While both authentic and plagal modes had the same final, they each had a different reciting tone. In the authentic modes, the reciting tone was mostly a fifth higher than the final while in the plagal modes it was usually a third above the final i.e.

```
                      F              RT
Authentic Mode:   D   e   f   g   A   b   c   D
                              F              RT
Plagal Mode:          a   b   c   D   e   F   g   a
```

This gave to melodies in the plagal mode a variation of colour and emphasis, which both complimented yet at the same time contrasted with those melodies sung in the equivalent authentic modes. The authentic modes were ascribed odd numbers beginning with I, while the plagal modes were ascribed even numbers. The first and second modes were therefore the authentic and plagal forms of the original mode Protus, the third and fourth the authentic and plagal forms of the mode Deuterus, and so on.

Later theorists went on to ascribe a series of Greek names to the modes, the D mode being called Dorian, the E mode Phrygian, the F mode Lydian and the G mode Mixolydian. The plagal form was then distinguished by the addition of the prefix 'Hypo', so the system of eight modes appears as shown in fig. 1.3.

Fig. 1.3: *The Eight Ecclesiastical Modes*

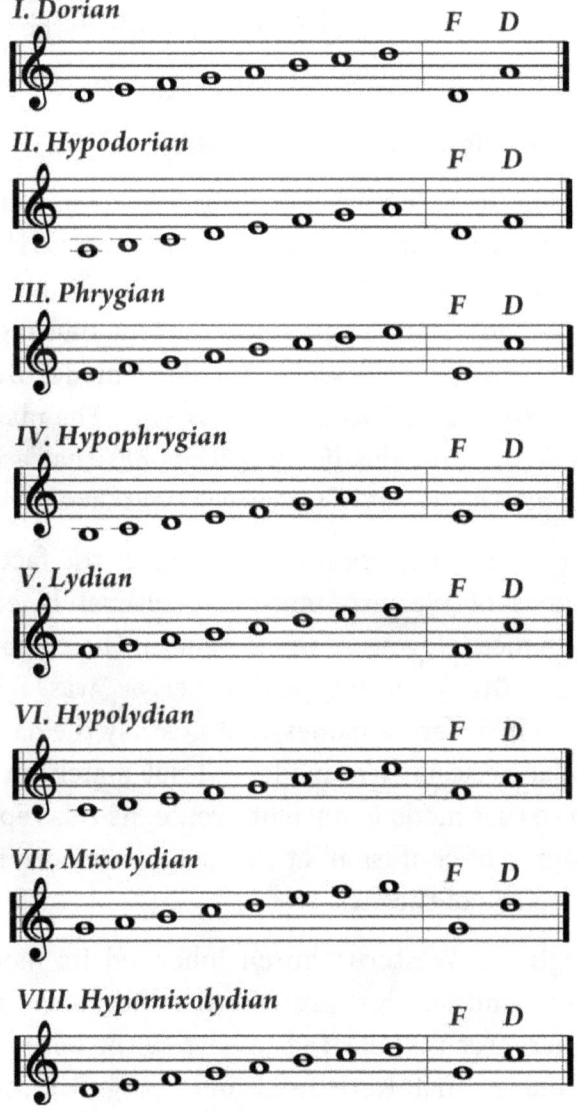

The process of transition from the modal system to the major and minor scale system that is more widely recognized today, represents a vast and complex study, one that cannot possibly be covered in this volume. However, it is important to observe that there is in some senses, a direct line of continuity between this ancient modal system and the scales that are generally used in the West today. This manifests principally in a general preference for the use of diatonic scales, of which the major and minor scales are two examples.

Ancient Greek origins of diatonic scales...

It is important to recognize however, that the ecclesiastical modes do not represent the point of origination of this line of continuity, but only the vehicle for its subsequent transmission and promulgation into the sphere of Western music generally. Indeed, to find the original source for these modes we need to look much further back into musical history. The main clue to the origins of these modes lies in the names that ascribed to them, which are the names of various ancient Greek tribes.

This represents a direct acknowledgement of the fact that the diatonic modes of Western music are ultimately of ancient Greek provenance. However, when naming these modes after their original Greek prototypes, an error was made that ascribed to them different names, that is to say the names given to a particular ecclesiastical mode, did not match up with the name given to that mode in ancient Greece. As this represents a potential source of confusion, at this stage, no more is needed than an awareness of the fact.

Now although the Western church inherited its modes from ancient Greek music, this process of inheritance was very selective. There was no felt need to borrow the entire roster of scales and modes that were used and recognized in ancient Greek music. If that need had been felt, then the course of Western musical history may have turned out to be very different. Primarily this is because along with diatonic scales, the musicians of ancient Greece also used *chromatic* and *enharmonic* scales, whose profiles were radically different to the diatonic scale, so different in fact, that even today nobody is quite sure how these chromatic and enharmonic scales were actually used, or indeed, how they originated.

The musicians of ancient Greece also enjoyed the use of a veritable wealth and abundance of possibilities in terms of what can best be described as a process of fine-tuning, that is to say the tuning of the notes of the scale in such a way as to create a tangible sense of mood, atmosphere and feeling. An example of this has already been given in the form of Archytas diatonic scale.

In the West however, due to the influence of the church, only one type of fine tuning was officially sanctioned, which was Pythagorean tuning, a method which, for the musicians of ancient Greece at least, probably represented no more than the most basic tuning, felt suitable perhaps, only for those novices just learning to play a musical instrument. In this way, one of the fabulous features of ancient Greek musical art simply disappeared from sight. However, fortunately there is enough knowledge and information available about ancient Greek music and its scales, which at least enable some of the main principles of this art to be recovered.

The schism between scale and tuning...

The word 'tuning' therefore proves very relevant to the investigation, simply because it possesses certain connotations today, among which are the curious sense of an inherent schism between a musical scale, and the way in which that scale is subsequently tuned. Implicit to this is the idea that the tuning process is secondary to the musical scale that is used.

This assumption, that the musical scale and the way in which it is tuned, refer to separate domains is deeply ingrained today, so deeply in fact, that it never seems to be questioned. There is the musical scale and there is the way in which that scale is then tuned. In terms of the latter, there are numerous options available, among which are Pythagorean tuning, equally tempered tuning, just tuning, mean-tone temperament, etc., etc.. The availability of these different types of tuning serves to reinforce the rational position that scale and tuning are thereby separate domains.

In this case therefore, there is the implicit assumption that the scale is a 'given object' to which a process of tuning is then applied. However, if this is true, what is the nature of that object that is referred to as a musical scale? Where did it come from? How did it arise? Because if the scale is taken to be a *given* object of our musical experience, then it almost seems as if the scale just appeared, fully-formed, from nowhere.

The philosophy of Aristoxenus of Tarentum…

This sense of the musical scale as a 'given', has its roots in a philosophy of music that goes right back to ancient Greece, some three or four centuries before the Christian era, in the form of the figure Aristoxenus of Tarentum (fl. 335 BC). A one-time pupil of Aristotle, Aristoxenus was a prolific author, reputed to have penned over four hundred books. Unfortunately, none of these have survived bar an important treatise on music *The Elements of Harmony*.

This treatise represents a remarkable exposition of Aristoxenus' own unique take on the music of his day. The word 'take' is quite aptly used here, because Aristoxenus was very careful not to simply pass on what was then considered received wisdom. Indeed, he had no qualms whatsoever in challenging that body of accepted wisdom and developing in its stead, an entirely new approach to the understanding of music in general.

Central to Aristoxenus' approach was the placing of a great premium upon musical experience. Seeing the domain of musical experience to be ultimately self-qualifying, Aristoxenus argued that many of the elements of a coherent and rational theory of music could be based on no more than a process of direct observation of that experience. For the time, this undoubtedly represented a unique position, one which even today, is probably still capable of generating fresh insights. Indeed, once Aristoxenus' position has been fully appreciated, it then becomes difficult to see the matter in any other way.

A good example of a self-qualifying musical experience is the process of tuning a stringed instrument, such as the ancient Greek lyre for example. This was always was done by ear, a process that does not generally prove problematic, because a good tuner will be perfectly capable of recognizing a properly tuned octave, perfect fifth and perfect fourth, which are the most important intervals of the tuning process.

Furthermore, any discerning musician will soon work out that these intervals are related in certain ways. Studying these relationships they may even discover that the interval of a perfect fourth, when added to the interval of a perfect fifth makes an octave. Similarly, a perfect fourth when *subtracted* from a perfect fifth leaves a whole tone. In this case therefore, two already qualified elements, the perfect fifth and fourth, may be used to define and delineate the existence of a third. Now as a result of applying this direct evidential approach to a process of musical enquiry, many basic questions about music and musical scales can be easily answered, such as:

What is an octave? An octave is the sum of a perfect fifth and fourth.

What is a perfect fifth? A fifth is the deficiency of the octave and a perfect fourth.

What is a whole tone? A whole tone is the interval left over when a fourth is subtracted from a fifth.

What is a semitone? A semitone is the interval left over when a ditone (two whole tones) is subtracted from a perfect fourth.

Observe how this line of thinking inevitably leads towards the point where a usable musical scale can be formulated. To be able do this furthermore, there is no need for the use of complex theories involving mathematics, or the use of cumbersome and often lengthy note-ratios that are often found in some music theory textbooks. Indeed, against the specific domain of practical musical experience, such features come across as being no more than mere abstractions.

A commonwealth of musical experience...

In pointing to the self-qualifying nature of musical experience, Aristoxenus' theories are still capable of helping us to understand just why, throughout the world, musicians have often made such similar choices in terms of the musical intervals used for the process of developing and building musical scales.

The octave for example, is recognized and used as a repeating pitch cycle in musical scales all over the world. The powerful consonant intervals of the perfect fifth and the perfect fourth are also universally recognized, intervals which like the octave, were probably originally discovered through no more than a process of happenstance i.e. the newly discovered combination of notes just sounded good together.

Furthermore, when the perfect fourth and fifth are placed into the octave, a simple four note structure composed of two perfect fourths separated by a whole tone is arrived at, a structure that we find embedded in musical scales the world over. These three intervals moreover, are the very fundamentals implicated by Aristoxenus in his investigations of the musical language of ancient Greece.

What explains this powerful sense of commonality, is not the existence of some kind of advanced acoustic science based on mathematics, but no more than a corpus of musical experience that all musicians ultimately share, both now and throughout the ages; a corpus of experience that instinctively leads musicians along similar pathways, and to arrive at similar scale structures. In tapping into this corpus of essential musical experience, Aristoxenus uniquely demonstrated that it could be used as a direct and viable pathway to a certain type of musical knowledge.

2 Pythagorean Arithmetic

The ingenuity of Aristoxenus' empirical approach to the study of musical scales is self-evident. However, although his ideas are widely regarded even to this day, it is doubtful that Aristoxenus can be claimed to have provided the last word on the subject. This is because his stance was clearly a reactive one, which means to say that it depended for its impact upon the existence of an already established body of knowledge.

Being aware of this body of knowledge, offering as it were, a springboard against which he could resist, there were certain questions that Aristoxenus did not care to answer. A good example of this is the question of intervallic quality. Why are some musical intervals concordant and others discordant? Although Aristoxenus recognized this dualistic distinction of intervallic quality, he did not attempt to explain the reasons for it[1]. Possibly, this is because so far as musical experience is concerned, the fact of intervallic quality is already self-evident. Therefore it may be taken to be a given.

---

[1] Mathiesen (1999), *Apollo's Lyre - Greek Music and Music Theory in Antiquity and the Middle Ages*, p. 310 – 11.

However if accepted as a *given*, this is tantamount to an evasion of those more searching questions that seek out a tangible cause for intervallic quality. Just why do two notes separated by an octave sound *so* similar to one another, that to the ear, they sound like the same note, but occurring on different pitch levels? Is this not one of the most mysterious and unsolvable paradoxes of our musical experience? What is the explanation for it? Taking the experience of the octave as being a *given* is clearly not enough.

Pythagorean number lore...

Seeking answers to some of these questions, inevitably leads to the consideration of another influential ancient Greek figure, who in his time also made significant contributions to the realms of ancient Greek musical theory: the philosopher Pythagoras of Samos (approx. 570 - 495 BC). Although usually remembered for no more than the theorem that carries his name, Pythagoras taught a unique syncretism of subjects among which number, astronomy, geometry and music - later to become the quadrivium of classical education - played a key role. The influence of Pythagorean teachings on early Greek musical theory was considerable, establishing as it did, that distinct mathematical tenor which often accompanied subsequent explorations and investigations of musical scales and modes by other Greek theorists, writers and philosophers.

The students and followers of Pythagoras - the Pythagoreans - were particularly interested in numbers, not however envisioned at a quantitative level, but more specifically, at a qualitative level as a direct means for the expression of universal verities. Aristotle observed in this respect, that the Pythagoreans 'supposed the elements of numbers to be the elements of all things, and the whole heaven to be a musical scale and a number.'[2] The general knowledge and theories surrounding this subject came to be studied under the general mantle of what Plato later referred to in the Republic as the 'study of arithmetic'. Clearly this was not the arithmetic that is taught today in schools.

The numbers of the decade...

The Pythagoreans placed great emphasis on the numbers of the decade, the most important number of which was one, significant of the unity from which all other numbers were subsequently derived. The number one in this sense signified the first cause, the primal and unknowable essence of the universe from which everything else was believed to have originated.

An important feature of this study was the qualitative distinction between odd and even numbers. Even numbers were divisible by two, while odd numbers divided by the same number always yielded one extra. The decade therefore contained five odd numbers (1, 3, 5, 7 and 9) and five even numbers (2, 4, 6, 8, and 10). All of the odd numbers were considered male, the even numbers female. Accordingly, the number five, composed of the masculine odd number three and the female even number two, was therefore considered the number of marriage.

Within the terms of Pythagorean philosophy therefore, the words *even* and *odd* had similar meanings to the words yin and yang for the ancient Chinese philosophy of the Tao. Within Taoism the even numbers are considered yin, female and passive, the odd numbers yang, male and active. In this context therefore, *even* and *odd* were symbolic terms used to denote the

---

[2] Aristotle, *Metaphysics*, Book 1, Part 5.

dualistic expression of the first principle of Pythagorean teachings: the number one or monad.

However, discounting for a moment this sense of mystique that surrounded the study of numbers, it is equally clear that for every great civilization of the world, numbers themselves have provided a vital tool for contributing a sense of measure, order and organization without which, civilization could probably never have even existed. Indeed, Plato long ago observed that 'numerical division in all its variety can be usefully applied to every field of conduct'.[3] Seeing in those numbers a direct reflection of the universal order itself therefore, represented no more than an intuitive leap of the mind beyond the otherwise functional and utilitarian purposes that have always been served by numbers.

The Tetractys...

When studying ancient Greek musical scales through the available literature, the abundance of references to the symbolic figure known as the Pythagorean *Tetractys* are particularly notable. For this reason alone, it is necessary to become at least acquainted with such Pythagorean symbolism, in order that such references may be properly understood in their original context.

The Tetractys consisted of a simple triangular figure composed of ten pebbles or dots arranged in four rows, the uppermost row of which has one, the next row two, the third row three and the bottom row four dots. See Fig. 2.1 for an illustration of the Pythagorean Tetractys.

---

[3] Plato, *Laws*, 747.

Fig.2.1: *The Pythagorean Tetractys*

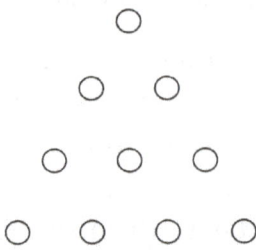

The sense of awe and veneration with which the Pythagoreans regarded the Tetractys is tangibly present in all written expositions of the subject. Moreover, it seems that for the Pythagoreans, the figure of the Tetractys embodied a profundity considered so great that all members of the Pythagorean fraternity were compelled to swear their oaths upon it. As a glyph moreover, it offered a visual summary of Pythagorean knowledge, comparable in its own way perhaps, to the Tree of Life diagram used by Hebrew Kabbalists. Consequently, the symbol of the Tetractys clearly possessed a significance upon multiple levels.

The four stages of creation...

One such level was as a symbolic form of representation of the numbers of the decade (1 – 10) which, for the Pythagoreans, signified the fundamental first causes of the universe. Another level of meaning was expressed by the four rows of dots which in one sense at least, signified the four stages of the creation of the known universe.

The logic of this is fairly easy to follow, without any necessary sacrifice of rationality to mysticism. No phenomenon could exist without an initial point of reference. The unitary point in this sense, thereby signified the very beginnings of the possibility for creation. However, a single point is as yet dimensionless, possessing as it does, the property of location but not extension. Hence, a second point is needed, thereby giving rise to the possibility of the line, drawn between two such points.

This line clearly represents a new unity, the first stage of the emergence of a determinate reality from an otherwise indeterminate potentiality. The line itself however, offers movement in only one dimension. As such, it is always limited without reference to something outside of it. This something is represented by a third dot, which thereby gives rise to the possibility of the plane, whose simplest form of expression is the triangle.

However the plane is also in a sense limited, having no real sense of depth. The latter only becomes possible through the use of a fourth dot in order to give rise to the possibility of the solid form, the simplest expression of which is the tetrahedron that uses four points of reference. In this way, the Tetractys was seen to embody the entire process of the creation of the three-dimensional world from nothing but an original, single point of reference.

For the Pythagoreans therefore, the process of universal genesis progressed through four successive stages, each stage yielding yet another dimension of manifestation. The Tetractys thus offered a certain pre-eminence to the numbers 1, 2, 3 and 4, as signifying the primary forces of the cosmic order. Consequently, the Pythagoreans associated with those four numerical terms certain elements, directions, colours, geometric figures, magnitudes, faculties of the soul, seasons of the year and so on.

Each such tetrad signified a particular domain of expression of the very same numerical principles, but operating on its own respective level. The symbol of the Tetractys consequently, was a symbolic point of economy, a succinct encapsulation of the essential knowledge that underpinned the Pythagorean worldview. In table 2 can be seen ten such sets of four that were important to the Pythagoreans.

Table 2: *Levels of the Pythagorean Tetractys*

Numbers:	One	Two	Three	Four
Elements:	Fire	Air	Water	Earth
Beings:	Seed	Length	Breadth	Thickness
Faculties:	Intellect	Knowledge	Opinion	Sensation
Age:	Infancy	Youth	Adulthood	Old Age
Magnitude:	Point	Line	Plane	Solid
Figure:	Tetrahedron	Octahedron	Icosahedron	Cube
Society:	Man	Family	Village	City
Season:	Spring	Summer	Autumn	Winter
Soul:	Spirited	Rational	Appetitive	Body

The Tetractys and music...

For the Pythagoreans, one of the most intriguing features of the Tetractys was its evident application to music, in particular the constructive role that it played in the process of musical scale generation. The fabled 'discovery' of the application of the Tetractys to music[4], was said to have occurred by way of an important discovery made by Pythagoras as he was walking past a blacksmith's shop.

Hearing the blacksmith at work, Pythagoras noticed that the notes produced by the blacksmith's hammers were in a harmonious relationship with one another. Suspecting that there might be a connection between the notes produced by the

---

[4] An account of which was given in the sixth chapter of the neo-Pythagorean philosopher Nicomachus of Gerasa's *Manual of Harmonics*.

hammers and their actual weight, Pythagoras went into the shop to investigate further. Weighing the hammers, he discovered that they were 6, 8, 9, and 12 pounds in weight respectively.

Pythagoras then observed that:

- the hammers that weighed 6 and 12 pounds produced the consonant interval of an octave;
- the hammers that weighed 6 and 9 pounds produced the consonant interval of a perfect fifth;
- the hammers that weighed 12 and 9 pounds produced the consonant interval of a perfect fourth;
- the hammers that weighed 8 and 9 pounds however, produced a discordant interval of a whole tone.

Now although the facts of this anecdotal story do not stand up to scientific scrutiny, the mere existence of the story serves to highlight the fact that Pythagoras was accredited as having been the first person in history to discover a causal link between the quality of a musical interval, in terms of consonance and dissonance, and the ratio of that interval.[5]

Pythagorean note ratios…

In this sense, the numbers of the Tetractys were thereby seen to sanction certain musical intervals, in particular those whose ratios remained within the bounds of the numbers of the tetrad. Among these were the intervals referred to today as the three perfect consonances, called *symphonies* in ancient Greece. These

---

[5] Although ancient Greek theorists had no such means to measure frequencies, they nonetheless suspected that the pitch of a note was determined by its frequency i.e. the speed of pulsation of the air.

were:

The octave (i.e. note C to note C1) which the Greeks called *diapason* - ratio 2/1.

The perfect fifth (i.e. note C to note G), which the Greeks called *diapente* - ratio 3/2.

The perfect fourth (i.e. note C to note F), which the Greeks called *diatessaron* - ratio 4/3.

All other intervals recognized in antiquity – such as the whole tone of ratio 9/8 - were accordingly regarded to be dissonant.

Ratios as tools for acoustic investigations...

For the Pythagoreans this represented a monumental discovery, since it showed that the numbers that were believed to regulate the harmony of the cosmos, also proscribed the foundations and limits for musical harmony. Indeed, since Pythagoras' initial discoveries, the ratio itself has since become a vital tool for investigations into the nature of acoustic reality.

For any person interested in the subject of musical scales therefore, it would be wise to become familiar with the use of ratios, as well as developing an awareness of some of the various simple mathematical operations practiced and used by ancient Greek musical theorists and mathematicians. It is also necessary to become aware of modern conventions with regard to the treatment and representation of these ratios within a written format.

One of the main reasons for this is that today, the musician is not generally required to be the pioneering scientist of their own art. Generally, musicians leave the more scientific matters to acousticians, physicists who may or may not themselves be musicians. Ordinarily this is perfectly acceptable, until of course the musician takes the bold step of stepping outside of the conventions of their musical culture, and investigating either new possibilities, or ancient possibilities that have now been discarded and forgotten. If this is the case, then the musician thereby needs to re-educate themselves and take back for themselves the prerogative that has been so lazily handed over to the sciences.

The composition of ratios...

Any ratio consists of two numbers, a numerator, which is customarily placed at the top of the ratio and a denominator that is placed at the bottom. However, when representing the ratio in a passage of text, the above mode of representation tends to be replaced by a form in which the numerator comes first, the denominator last. Between the two numbers is then placed either a diagonal line or a colon. Therefore the ratio of three to two can be represented either as 3/2 or alternatively 3:2.

Of the two numbers belonging to a ratio, the numerator designates the frequency of the upper note, as relative to the frequency of the lower note. Therefore the ratio 3/2 signifies that the upper note has three oscillations for every two oscillations of the lower note. In this sense, the absolute measurement of the frequencies of the two notes is unimportant. What is important is their *relationship* to one another. For this reason, to discover the ratio between the frequencies of two notes, the vibration numbers designating those frequencies are always reduced down by their common factors. Therefore if the frequencies of the two notes are 256Hz and 192 Hz, the relationship between them is expressed by the ratio 4/3, the simplest possible way of representing their essential frequency relationship.

Harmonic relationships...

Another importance of the ratio is that it shows that so far as musical languages are concerned, a note itself is never more than just a sound. As a mere sound, a single note can have no meaning or significance whatsoever, aside from indicating the presence of a certain type of mechanical disturbance of the surrounding atmosphere. Admittedly, as a type of sound, the note is rather special, having certain properties of regularity, stability and periodicity which commend its use in a musical context, As a part of a musical language however, a note can only acquire a meaning and a significance when it is brought into relationship with other such notes. Each such relationship will count as new unity, that is to say a tangible identity that subsumes the two notes brought into such a relationship. These identities are called musical intervals.

The determination of the character and quality of the identity occurs by way of the ratio, that is to say the mathematical relationship between the frequencies of the two tones. When that relationship is a simple one, the interval has the quality of consonance, while if a complex one, the interval has the quality of a dissonance. The ratio itself therefore, designates the precise *harmonic relationship* between the two notes. What this means is that the frequencies of the two notes are always heard and compared as multiples of a common unity. This unity is therefore the factor that unites the two tones into that harmonic relationship. Therefore in the case of the ratio 15/8, the number 1 in this instance, refers to the common unity of which both numerator and denominator are multiples.

In this sense, musical languages usually tend to be built upon the resonant properties and qualities of such harmonic relationships. Initially, this probably only happened because for the ear, harmonic relationships stand out like stars in the dark canopy of the night shy. The fundamental governing principle is always unity, for without a sense of a common unity, no harmonic relationship could exist.

The numbers of the Pythagorean decade are therefore musically significant because they generate the most important, usable harmonic relationships. Their usability in this respect, is generally assessed and determined by the ear, in the sense that the simpler the harmonic relationship i.e. the closer to unity, the more concordant the resulting interval. The simplicity of the relationship in this case, seems to be the ear's measure of the closeness of that relationship to a state of unity. This latter state is therefore represented musically by the ratio 1/1, which thereby signifies an absolute, complete and total expression of unity, that is to say the most perfect state of concord.

Ratios as designating note positions...

Another use of note ratios was in order to express the precise position of a single note in the octave. In this context the lower number signifies the lower note of the octave, the upper number the position of the note within the octave. In this sense, every possible ratio designates the precise position of a note within the octave, a musical scale being envisaged as a sum of such positions.

Ancient Greek theorists therefore, often represented their scales by a numerical series, in which the relationships between individual tones could therefore be expressed as ratios. A good example of this is Ptolemy's equable diatonic scale which he represented by the number series 18 – 20 – 22 – 24 – 27 – 30 – 33 – 36. The numbers 36/18 in this sense, signify the octave, while the other numbers signify the positions of the individual notes of the scale within the octave. These positions would therefore be defined by the series of ratios 10/9; 11/9; 4/3; 3/2; 5/3; 11/6 and 2/1. This process is illustrated in Fig. 2.2 in which the octave space is represented as a straight line stretched between the numbers 18 and 36.

Fig. 2.2: *Ptolemy's equable diatonic scale expressed as whole numbers*

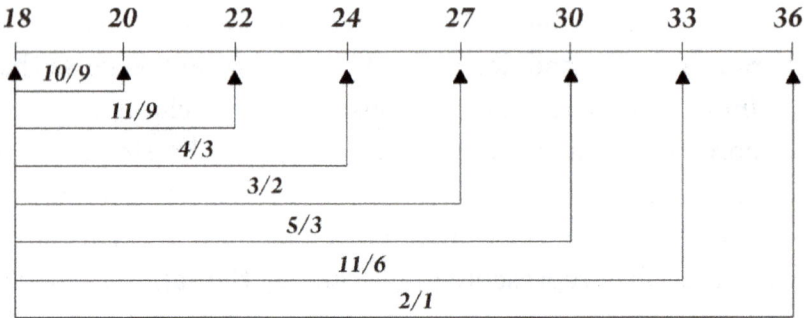

Common operations...

Sometimes two intervals need to be added together in order to work out the interval that represents their sum. In this case:

- the numerator of the first ratio is multiplied by the numerator of the second ratio,
- the denominator of the first ratio is multiplied by the denominator of the second ratio,
- the common factors of the numbers are then eliminated in order to reduce the ratio down to the use of the simplest numbers possible.

Here are three examples of this.

In a) the intention is to discover the sum of the two intervals of a perfect fifth (ratio 3/2) and a diatonic semitone (16/15). The result in this case is the harmonic minor sixth (8/5).

In b) the intention is to discover the sum of a harmonic major third (5/4) and harmonic minor third (6/5), the result of which is a perfect fifth (3/2).

In c) the intention is to discover the sum of a whole tone (9/8) and septimal augmented second (7/6), the result being a septimal augmented third (21/16).

a) $\quad \dfrac{3}{2} \text{ plus } \dfrac{16}{15} = \dfrac{3 \times 16}{2 \times 15} = \dfrac{48}{30} = \dfrac{8}{5}$

b) $\quad \dfrac{5}{4} \text{ plus } \dfrac{6}{5} = \dfrac{5 \times 6}{4 \times 5} = \dfrac{30}{20} = \dfrac{3}{2}$

c) $\quad \dfrac{9}{8} \text{ plus } \dfrac{7}{6} = \dfrac{9 \times 7}{8 \times 6} = \dfrac{63}{48} = \dfrac{21}{16}$

Another common operation is to subtract a smaller from a larger interval in order to work out the interval that represents their difference. In this case:

- the numerator of the first ratio is multiplied by the denominator of the second ratio,
- the denominator of the first ratio is multiplied by the numerator of the second ratio.
- the common factors of the numbers are then eliminated in order to reduce the ratio down to the use of the simplest numbers possible.

Here are three examples of this.

In a) the intention is work out the interval that represents the difference between the perfect fifth (3/2) and diatonic semitone (16/15), which as the example shows, is a harmonic augmented fourth (45/32).

In b) the intention is to work out the interval that represents the difference between the harmonic major third (5/4) and the harmonic minor third (6/5) the resulting being the minor diatonic semitone of 25/24.

In c) the intention is to work out the interval that represents the difference between the septimal augmented second (7/6) and the diatonic whole tone (9/8), the result being the septimal diesis (28/27).

a) $\quad \dfrac{3}{2} \text{ minus } \dfrac{16}{15} = \dfrac{3 \times 15}{2 \times 16} = \dfrac{45}{32}$

b) $\quad \dfrac{5}{4} \text{ minus } \dfrac{6}{5} = \dfrac{5 \times 5}{4 \times 6} = \dfrac{25}{24}$

c) $\quad \dfrac{7}{6} \text{ minus } \dfrac{9}{8} = \dfrac{7 \times 8}{6 \times 9} = \dfrac{56}{54} = \dfrac{28}{27}$

The monochord...

The discoveries made by Pythagoras with regard to musical ratios were all directly verifiable using the instrument favored for this purpose, the monochord. Consisting of a single string stretched over a sounding box provided with a movable bridge that could be used to stop the string at any point, this was the perfect instrument for acoustic experimentation. Through use of this instrument the mathematical ratios implied by the Tetractys could not only be demonstrated, but also played, heard and experienced. When for example, the bridge was placed at the exact centre point of the string the note was heard to rise an octave. In other words, as the string length was halved, the frequency of the note was thereby doubled.

When studying pitch through such methods however, it is difficult to get very far without establishing a clear focal point, a fixed point of reference that lay at the very heart of the pitch continuum. Thinking back to the Tetractys, this fixed point would represent the number one, the first point from which the creation of the known universe was considered to begin. In this way, this central point of the pitch continuum could be envisaged as defining the very centre of a great circle, all around it on the perimeter lying the undivided bounds of the pitch continuum as signified by the string as a whole.

The note practically used for this purpose was the mése, or 'tone of the middle string' on the lyre, the central note around which the entire ancient Greek musical cosmos revolved. In this sense, the mése performed a similar function to the Kung of the ancient Chinese tone system, the central note that acted as the fundamental generator for all other note relationships.

In Indian music, note Sa, symbolized by the piercing cry of the peacock, performed a similar role. Consequently, while the other notes of the scale were considered analogous to the various parts of the human body, note Sa was considered analogous to the power that moved the body viz., the human soul. The nearest equivalent to such a central note in our modern Western musical theory would therefore probably be note 'Middle C', the fundamental reference tone for the entire Western tonal system.

A convenient position for the mése was therefore exactly halfway along the string of the monochord. This enabled the study of pitch relationships both rising up and falling down from the central note of the mése. Being located halfway along the string, the mése thus stood in an octave relationship to the string's fundamental. In this respect, clear recognition was given to the unique property of the octave, leading as it does to a perception of the same note, but manifesting on a higher or lower level of the pitch continuum.

This perception in its turn was seen to be rooted in mathematics, in particular the mathematics of the Tetractys in the form of the ratio 2:1. Being the simplest ratio involving unlike numbers, this relationship was therefore seen to be the closest to a sense of absolute unity, as would be represented by the ratio of 1/1 – the absolute concordance of tones that is today called the interval of the prime.

The ancient Greek double octave...

A single octave was therefore conceived of as a circle – one turn of a spiral that emanated from the central tone of the mésē. Placing the mésē at the top of the octave circle shows that a single circle is not sufficient. This is because proceeding round the circle clockwise, a rise of pitch is signified, while proceeding around the circle in an anti-clockwise direction a fall of pitch is signified.

The recognition of the simple fact of a single octave therefore, automatically implicated the much fuller and more complete expression of a double octave. This idea can be appreciated when the octave circle is mapped onto a monochord: a clockwise revolution manifests as a rising octave which implicates a halving of the length of the string, while an anticlockwise direction manifests as a falling octave which implicates a doubling of the length of the string. Hence the necessity for establishing a central note that lay at the exact midpoint between the rising and falling octaves.

This is portrayed diagrammatically in Fig. 2.3 in which the mésē is shown standing at the center of the double octave circle and at opposite sides of the perimeter of the circles designating the upper and lower octaves.

Fig. 2.3: *The Ancient Greek Double Octave*

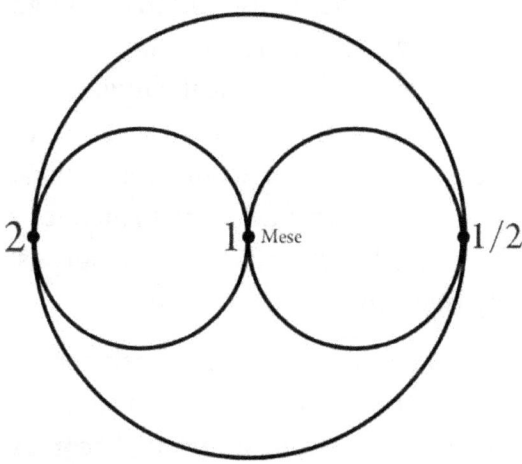

The monochord has since become one of the prime tools for acoustic investigations into the nature and character of harmonic relationships (musical intervals). It also provided a convenient and useful pedagogical tool for the demonstration of harmonic relationships.

The general key to such investigations has always been the numbers of the Pythagorean decade. Each number is conceptualized as a divisor, each division yielding the basis for an entirely new set of harmonic relationships. In this way, harmonic relationships may be envisaged as growing like a tree, beginning with a root that is the original unity and then gradually proliferating through the application of ever higher numerical principles.

That the various fractional parts of the string yielded by the treatment of each number as a divisor, exactly correspond to the natural modes of vibration of the string responsible for the production of those partials of the fundamental tone that are present and accountable in the harmonic series, proved to be a happy coincidence.

This particular coincidence has no doubt preserved the relevance of these acoustic investigations throughout the ages, for the principles revealed are clearly just as important for the further development of the musical language today, as they were back in the times of ancient Greece. In this sense, the original numbers themselves become the permanent symbols and beacons of those natural acoustic principles that each age and culture may draw from for the specific purpose of renewing and revitalizing their own musical languages.

Consequently, the study of ancient Greek musical scales and modes has a vital relevance even to today's generation of musicians. For through this study it becomes possible to reacquaint ourselves with these natural acoustic principles. In this respect, nothing much has changed since then. All that has changed is the cultural terms of reference. For example, instead of discussing the harmonic applications of the septenary, musicians now refer to the role of the seventh harmonic, and its application to the domain of septimal harmony. Although the terms of reference are therefore different, the fundamental principles remain and have remained the same throughout the ages.

3 Genesis of the Greek Scale System

The respective approaches to the theory of musical scales made by the Pythagoreans on the one hand and Aristoxenus on the other, have often been taken to refer to diametrically opposing positions. Whether agreeing with either of these positions, or not as the case may be, it is fascinating to see how, throughout the history of music, they have often been played off against one another.

On the Pythagorean side it was observed that when musical tones are brought into a relationship with one another as determined by a simple ratio, that the human ear is capable of immediately recognizing this relationship. In this sense, the numerical ratio is therefore acting as cause, for an experiential effect perceived as the aural quality of that interval.

On the Aristoxenian side however, it was observed that for the human ear, all of this is self-evident. Therefore there is no real need to *know* that the ratio of the octave is 2/1 to perceive it as being such. The octave is a self-evident and self-qualifying fact of our musical perception, irrespective of any ratio that might be attributed to or seen to be connected with that perception. Indeed, Aristoxenus recognized that there will always be a certain indefinable region, zone or margin within which two notes will still be perceived as being an octave apart. As such, practical musical experience seemed to implicate a certain set of variables that supporters of the ratio as the final arbiter of musical experience did not care to recognize.

Modern Western equal temperament in this sense, relying as it does on the existence of such marginal zones, therefore represents an ultimate victory for the Aristoxenian point of view. Symptomatic of this perhaps, is the observation that the note ratios of the Pythagoreans have consequently now all but disappeared from our musical textbooks. At least until relatively recently, where a resurgence of interest is now beginning to reassert itself.

Reconciling the viewpoints of Aristoxenus and Pythagoras...

Connected with this resurgence is the awareness of a point where both of these arguments may be reconciled and ultimately synthesized into a higher viewpoint. Integral to this awareness is the observation that the ratio cannot be ignored forever, because ultimately it is the ratio that creates the relationship between the two tones that the ear itself recognizes. Once this recognition has become crystallized into an identifiable experience, then perhaps it may then be taken as a given.

A useful point of comparison is the visual form of a square. Everybody can recognize a square by eye alone. There is no need to measure the proportions of the lines to know that a given shape implies a square. The lines may not be exactly equal, but the *implication* of a square can still be recognized. In this context, the shape of the square may be taken to be a given object of our visual experience. However ultimately, what qualifies the shape of the square is the mathematical proportion between its four composite lines. A mathematically perfect square therefore, the model or archetype upon which all squares are based, is one in which the four lines are exactly equal in length.

The same argument can be applied to the interval of the octave. Aural recognition of an octave is not difficult, even if the two notes are slightly out of tune with one another. When they are slightly out of tune, the ear then recognizes the *implication* of the octave. However, the perfect model of the octave, the ideal upon which all octaves are based, is one in which the frequency of the fundamentals of the two tones are in an exact 2/1 relationship with one another.

In this sense, the viewpoints of Pythagoras and Aristoxenus are not really opposite to one another, but complimentary. Extreme positions therefore, only seem to arise when only one of these two viewpoints is recognized, usually at the direct expense of the other. For in the former case, this may lead to a pursuit of mathematical purity and elegance that becomes increasingly abstract and ultimately, irrelevant to the realities of musical experience. A good example of this, to be considered later in this book, is the divergent opinions on how the quartertone intervals of the enharmonic scale should be tuned. Clearly, these quartertone intervals are so small, that it is doubtful that the ear could detect any difference between the way in which they are tuned.

In the latter case, this may lead to a loss of knowledge of the fundamental mathematical principles that underlie the architecture of those structures called musical scales. This in turn may lead to an unquestioning acceptance of certain conventions that are justified on no more grounds than that our experience casts up those conventions as being somehow 'natural', 'normal' or 'given'. A lazy acceptance of the equally tempered twelve-tone scale as being 'the scale' of Western music is a good example of this.

In this context, it might be significant that, according to Plutarch's *On Osiris and Isis,* Pythagoras was received, taught and trained at the Egyptian temple. Here Pythagoras no doubt learned about the importance of these fundamental mathematical principles and how, when applied to music, they were capable of creating the architectural foundations for a musical language that was grounded in a universal sense of harmony, balance and proportion. At this level therefore, there never was a schism between a musical scale and how it is tuned, for the scale and the tuning were at one.

The four stringed lyre...

The musical scales that the West indirectly inherited from ancient Greek music did not just suddenly appear. Clearly, a process of continual musical development took place, assisted no doubt, by the periodic assimilation of certain elements from other musical cultures. Indeed, the Greeks openly acknowledged that they received many of their musical influences from other cultures.

The lyre for example, an instrument that became the very icon of ancient Greek music itself, is clearly visible in the decorative art and wall paintings of cultures such as Mesopotamia and Egypt. Often, such lyres are shown with few strings, showing that these early styles of music must have placed great emphasis on simplicity and directness of expression.

Indeed, the first century Greek historian Diodorus Siculus, who attributed the invention of the Egyptian lyre to Thoth, the Egyptian equivalent of Hermes, claimed that originally lyres had but three strings, the acute string of which was consecrated to the summer, the grave to the winter and the mean to the spring.[6]

In common with such prototypes, it seems that early Greek lyres also had but few strings. Confirmation of this view is given by the fifth century Roman author Theodosius Macrobius who reported that they had only four strings, which were again, consecrated to the seasons of the year.[7] This mention of the seasons by both writers clearly places the lyre being spoken of, more into a symbolic, rather than literal perspective.

As the cosmic order was supported and maintained by four principles, represented at their respective levels by the four elements, the four seasons and the four numbers of the Tetractys, it was perhaps inevitable that the archetypal lyre had but four strings, each string consecrated to a particular season. Music in this sense, as represented by the four stringed lyre, echoed the harmony of the four elements, or indeed the passage of the four seasons.

The tuning of the lyre...

If the lyre did have but four strings, what kind of musical scale was used? A clue is given by Nicomachus' (60 – 120 AD) in his *Manual of Harmonics* where he observes that the four strings of the lyre were tuned in accordance with the symbolic numbers of the Tetractys.

The sense of this can be grasped by recalling, for the moment,

---

[6] Diodorus Siculus, *Lacus Curtius*, Book I, 16.

[7] Macrobius, *Saturnalia*, 1.19.

the various divisions of the string of the monochord, as they proceed in accordance with these symbolic numbers. The number one produces the fundamental (fig. 3.1a) derived from the vibrations of the string as a whole; the number two produces the interval of the octave (fig. 3.1b) arising from a division of the string into two parts; the number three the interval of the perfect fifth (fig. 3.1c) arising from a division of the string into three parts and the number four the interval of the perfect fourth (fig. 3.1d) arising from a division of the string into four parts. These four stages are illustrated in fig. 3.1.

Fig 3.1: *First Four Divisions of the Monochord*

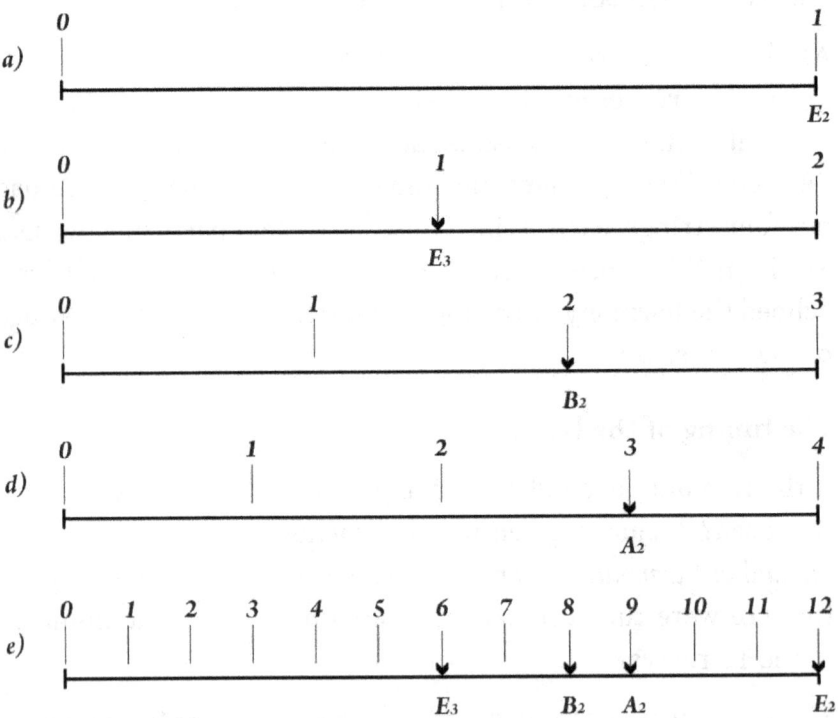

In terms of the four stringed lyre therefore, the two outer strings were tuned an octave apart, while the two middle strings were tuned to the perfect fifth (3/2) and fourth (4/3). In fig. 3.2 this tuning is shown, note E being used as no more than a convenient reference point.

Fig. 3.2: *Tuning of the Four Stringed Lyre*

Note:	E_2	A_2	B_2	E_3
Ratio:	1/1	4/3	3/2	2/1
Whole Number:	6	8	9	12

This gives the impression that the earliest Greek scale was tritonic. However, observe the series of numbers in the third row of the illustration. These are also the numbers that represented the relative weights of the blacksmith's hammers in pounds, implicated by Pythagoras in his 'discovery' of the ratios of the three perfect consonances - these being 6, 8, 9 and 12 pounds.

The usefulness of this number series is that it enabled the ratios of all of the intervals between the four notes of the scale to be expressed in simple whole numbers. Therefore the interval of the octave can be expressed by the ratio 12:6, the perfect fifth by the ratio of 9:6 and the perfect fourth by the ratio of 8:6. See fig. 3.1e for the way in which these numbers apply to the divisions of the monochord.

Also seen to be significant was the fact that eight represented the geometric mean and nine the arithmetic mean of the numbers six and twelve. Furthermore, 12:8 and 9:6 were related as geometric mean. The four stringed lyre as tuned in this fashion, therefore represented the perfect symbol for the Pythagorean cosmic order.

The pentatonic tuning of the lyre...

However, discounting this tuning of the lyre in what was probably a purely symbolic sense, it seems that for practical purposes, the four strings might even have been tuned to produce the notes of just a single tetrachord.[8] The two outer strings would therefore have been tuned a perfect fourth apart, while the two inner strings were then tuned to fill in the missing scale steps of the tetrachord.[9] If this is true, then the single tetrachord represented the earliest musical scale used by the Greeks.

However, another view, popularized by the ethnomusicologist Curt Sachs, is that a finger technique might have been used for stopping the strings in order to raise their pitch by a semitone or so.[10] If correct, this may indicate the possible use of pentatonic scales in ancient Greek music, in particular those of the major third variety, as used in various parts of Asia. This would make Nicomachus' scheme of tuning very practicable, despite the fact that, listening to modern lyre players stopping strings using this technique, shows that it has certain limitations. Although a change of pitch can be achieved, the resonant qualities of the note are significantly impaired.

The heptachord of Terpander...

However the four strings of the early lyre were actually tuned, according to both Plutarch and Nicomachus, the 7th century musician Terpander of Lesbos brought the number of strings on

---

[8] Godwyn, J. (1993) *The Harmony of the Spheres*, p. 194; Anderson. W. (1994), *Music and Musicians in Ancient Greece*, p. 47.

[9] The word tetrachord literally means 'four-stringed'.

[10] Curt Sachs (2008), *The Rise of Music in the Ancient World*, p. 206 – 210. See also R. P. Winnington-Ingram, (1956), *The Pentatonic Tuning of the Greek Lyre: A Theory Examined*.

the lyre from four up to seven.[11] This process was therefore accompanied by a significant expansion of scalar resources beyond the possible limits of a single tetrachord.

The logic behind that process of expansion was discussed by Aristotle who observed that Terpander's seven stringed lyre was tuned to produce a heptachord consisting of two tetrachords following the pattern of intervals: tone, tone and semitone in descending order.[12] See Fig. 3.3 for an illustration of this heptachord.

The heptachord of Terpander thus consisted of a lower tetrachord, which spanned the notes shown from A down to E.[13] Then there was the duplication of that tetrachord a fourth higher, which spanned the notes from D down to A. Observe that note A performed a special function in the heptachord, for it was the only note shared by both tetrachords, providing as it did the uppermost note for the lower tetrachord and the lowermost note for the upper tetrachord. Tetrachords connected by a common tone in this fashion were called conjunct tetrachords.

Furthermore, lying between the two tetrachords, exactly midway between the lowest and the highest notes of the heptachord, this connecting tone was called mésē meaning 'middle'. Although to musicians today the heptachord of Terpander seems strangely incomplete, at the time it no doubt represented a considerable expansion of pitch resources beyond the bounds of a single tetrachord.

---

[11] Plutarch, *On Music*; Nicomachus *Manual of Harmonics*, chap. 5.

[12] Aristotle, *Problems*, 19. 47.

[13] As conveniently expressed through Western notation.

Fig. 3.3: *The Heptachord of Terpander*

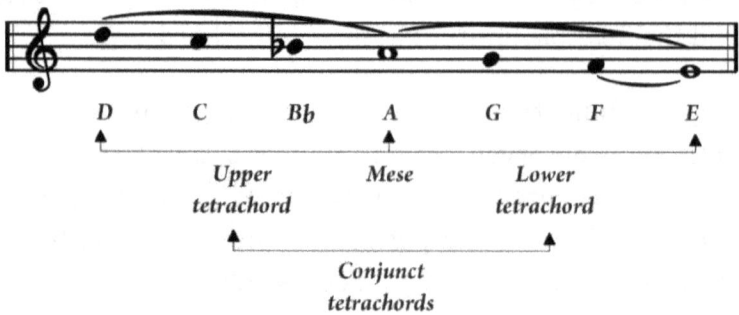

The heptachord also served to establish some of the principal characteristics of ancient Greek musical scales thereafter, these primarily being the recognition of the tetrachord as the main building block of the scale, together with a certain sense of reverence for the central tone of the ancient Greek gamut, the mésē, around which the other notes of the scale were seen to generally revolve.

Notes and planets...

Comparisons also came to be drawn between the seven tones of the heptachord and other sets of seven, such as the seven heavens whose spheres included the sun and moon along with the five wandering stars then recognized: Mercury, Venus, Mars, Jupiter and Saturn. The slowest and most remote wanderer Saturn, was compared to the longest string of the lyre, while the moon, the fastest moving sphere closest to the Earth, was compared to the shortest string.

In this way, a note was assigned to each of the seven planets that were considered to orbit the Earth in a series of concentric circles. Consequently, the heptachord itself was seen to represent a direct audible expression of the music of the spheres. Significantly, the central defining point of this harmony was represented by the mésē which, within the sevenfold cosmological scheme, was therefore consecrated to the sphere of the sun.

The Pythagorean octave scale...

Occupying the limited range of a minor seventh, the heptachord of Terpander seems conspicuously short of a complete octave. Indeed, according to Nicomachus, Pythagoras went on to add an eighth string to the lyre, thereby enabling the scale to be completed at the octave.[14]

In the process of doing so, the upper tetrachord was transposed up a tone to result in a new eight-note scale composed of two tetrachords separated by a tone of disjunction. Tetrachords related in this manner were referred to as disjunct tetrachords. This new eight stringed octave format is portrayed in fig. 3.4.

Fig. 3.4: *Pythagorean Octave Scale*

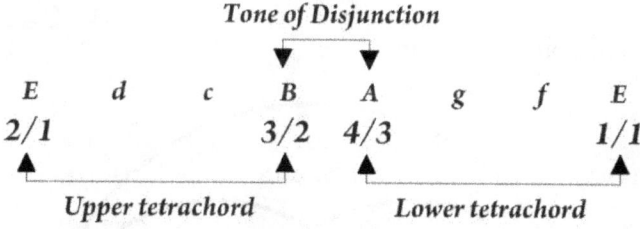

This octave scale offered two functional orders of notes – the fixed tones as portrayed in upper case note letters, and the movable tones as portrayed by lower case note letters.

The lower tetrachord contained two movable tones, which in the illustration are represented as notes F and G. Unlike the fixed notes that defined the tetrachordal framework, the positions of the movable notes could be changed, thereby

---

[14] Nicomachus, *Manual of Harmonics*, ch. 5

creating the possibility for different types of tetrachords.

The upper tetrachord, separated from the lower tetrachord by a tone of disjunction is constructed along similar lines, two movable notes whose positions could be altered, bounded by two fixed notes bearing a consonant perfect fourth relationship to one another.

Relationships between the four fixed tones...

Fig. 3.5 shows that the fixed tones generate four intervals in total. The extremes of the scale are related according to the octave ratio of 2/1, a perfect consonance. There are also two perfect fifths as represented by the *sesquialter* ratio 3/2, an exceedingly simple ratio yielding a powerful and perfect consonance. Therefore a perfect fifth up from the bottom note E produces note B, while a perfect fifth down from the top note E produces note A.

Fig. 3.5: *The Four Fixed Tones*

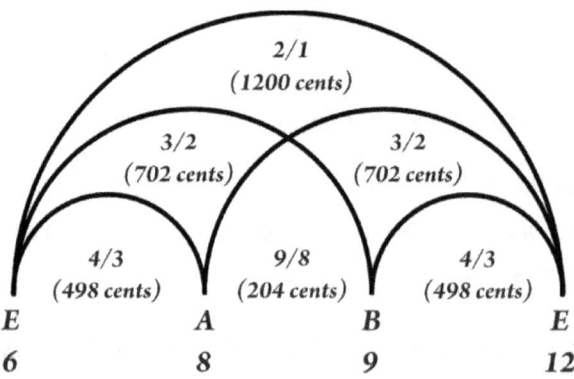

The two smaller arcs at the bottom similarly show the perfect fourth relationships, which define the bounds of the upper and lower tetrachords. These are expressions of the *epitritus* ratio 4/3, again a simple ratio that places the perfect fourth in the group of perfect consonances. There is the lower tetrachord bounded by the perfect fourth between the notes E and A and the upper tetrachord bounded by the perfect fourth between the notes B and E.

In this way, the four fixed tones create an interlocking grid of perfect consonant intervals, which then provide the unchanging backdrop to the mutable world of the movable tones - a world that utilized that less well defined, but superbly colorful and expressive space between each of the two tetrachords.[15]

The ancient Greek Dorian scale system...

One of the interesting features about the framework of the four fixed tones is that although composed of interlocking perfect consonants, they yield a dissonant interval of ratio 9/8 (204 cents) - the whole tone difference between the perfect fourth and perfect fifth. This whole tone, squeezed out as it were, through the recognizable difference between the perfect fifth and the perfect fourth, represented the very key to the Pythagorean approach to scale division.

Taking the whole tone between A and B as a basic measure, the theoretical positions for the other notes of the tetrachord can be deduced. Therefore coming down a whole tone from top E, note D is produced. Similarly, coming down a whole tone from note D note C is produced. This process cannot be continued however, because between C and B is an interval smaller than a whole tone. Having a ratio of 256/243 (90 cents), this interval was called the *limma*, this word meaning 'remainder'. In this way, a Dorian tetrachord was obtained as shown in fig. 3.6.

---

[15] Plutarch devotes a considerable part of a section (section 22) of his work On Music to a detailed discussion of these relationships and how they contribute to that sense of harmony expressed by the four fixed tones.

Fig. 3.6: *Ancient Greek Dorian Tetrachord (Upper)*

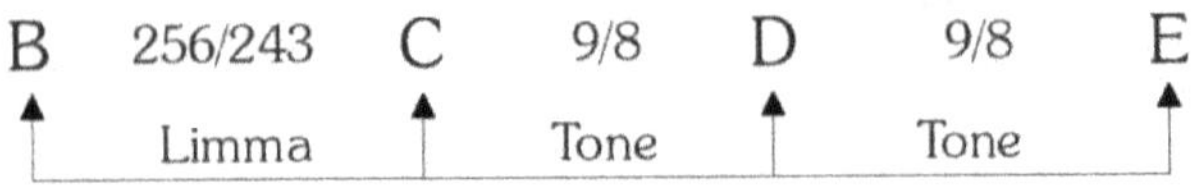

```
B   256/243   C    9/8    D    9/8    E
↑             ↑           ↑           ↑
└── Limma ────┴── Tone ───┴── Tone ───┘
```

The same process can then be repeated with respect to the lower tetrachord (fig. 3.7) which produces an identical division of the fourth into two whole tones and a limma.

Fig. 3.7: *Ancient Greek Dorian Tetrachord (Lower)*

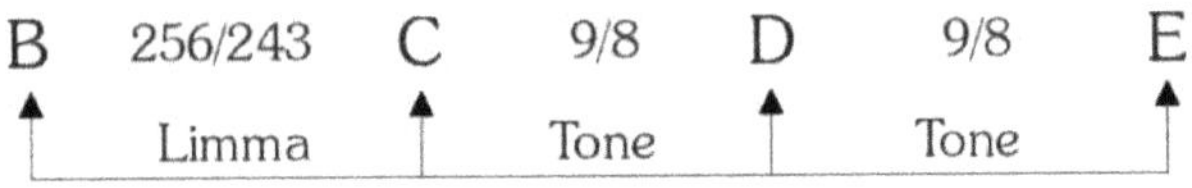

```
B   256/243   C    9/8    D    9/8    E
↑             ↑           ↑           ↑
└── Limma ────┴── Tone ───┴── Tone ───┘
```

The result is what came to be the basic scale system of ancient Greek music - the Dorian scale system as configured according to Pythagorean tuning. This scale system is portrayed in fig. 3.8:

Fig. 3.8: *Ancient Greek Dorian system*

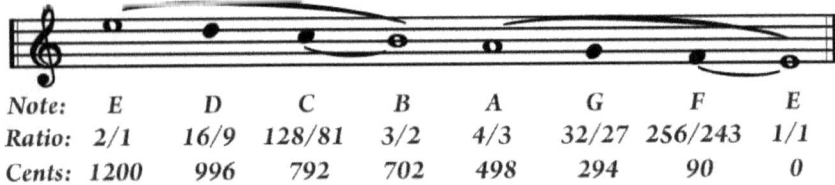

Note:	E	D	C	B	A	G	F	E
Ratio:	2/1	16/9	128/81	3/2	4/3	32/27	256/243	1/1
Cents:	1200	996	792	702	498	294	90	0

In its basic outlines this scale is very familiar to modern musicians, for it corresponds with the range of white keys on the keyboard starting from E and then proceeding stepwise down to note E on the octave below. The only difference with the modern equally tempered version of this scale, lies in the particular tuning of the individual notes. In the case of modern equal temperament these are rounded off to the nearest 100 cents. Comparing the Pythagorean tuning of the scale with equal temperament therefore, there is not a great deal of difference between them.[16] The biggest difference is one of ten cents, the difference between the equally tempered semitone and the limma. Observe that modern equal temperament in this sense, casts a distinctive shade of Pythagorean tuning on our entire musical output. This perhaps is not that surprising, because both scales come from exactly the same source.

The correlation between notes and strings of the lyre...

One of the interesting features encountered in the study of ancient Greek musical scales is the way scales were thought about and represented by theorists. Generally, they were envisaged with reference to the strings of an archetypal eight-stringed lyre. So close did this association come to be, that the notes themselves came to take their names from the strings on the lyre that sounded them. Therefore, one particular note of the scale was called lichanós, which means 'forefinger string'. However, for Greek musicians this also brought a particular note of the scale to mind, the note just below the mése.

However, a potentially confusing feature arises from the observation that the lowest pitched string of the lyre, was referred to as hypáte, which means *highest*. In this context, hypáte designated not the pitch of the note, but the position of the string relative to the performer. The highest pitched string tuned to the octave above hypáte was similarly called néte, meaning lowest or last string. The other string names, which will hereafter be used to name the notes of the ancient Greek scale, were as shown in table 3.

---

[16] In the modern tempered version all of the notes would be represented by round hundreds of cents.

Table 3: *Names of the Strings (Notes) of the Lyre*

Note	Number	String
E	First	Nétē (Last string)
D	Second	Paranétē (Next to last string)
C	Third	Trítē (Third string)
B	Fourth	Paramésē (Next to middle string)
A	Fifth	Mésē (Middle string)
G	Sixth	Lichanós (Forefinger string)
F	Seventh	Parhypátē (Next to the highest)
E	Eighth	Hypátē (Highest)

One of the conspicuous features of this scale is that there is no longer a true middle string. In his *Problems* Aristotle brought attention to this fact with the question: 'How can we speak of the mésē or middle note of a scale of eight notes?'[17] This lack of a true center is because the upper tetrachord descends from nétē to end with paramésē. Similarly, the lower tetrachord descends from mésē to end with hypátē.

Despite this loss of its central position in the scale, the mésē was still theoretically regarded as being the centre point of the scale due to its important melodic function, which will soon be discussed. The mésē also seems to have been used as a central reference point for tuning the lyre.[18] This process of tuning was accomplished by ear using the system of rising and falling perfect fourths or fifths.

Therefore starting from mésē, the next string to be logically tuned would be nétē, a perfect fifth above mésē. Next paramésē

---

[17] Aristotle, *Problems*, xix 26.

[18] Stefan Hagel (2010), *Ancient Greek Music: A Technical History*, p. 115.

could be tuned a perfect fourth below nétē. Then the player could return to the mésē and tune paranétē a perfect fourth above. The next string to be tuned could be lichanós, a perfect fifth below paranétē. From lichanós the player could then tune trítē a perfect fourth above lichanós. Parhypátē could then be tuned a perfect fifth below trítē. Finally, hypátē could be tuned an octave below nétē. Tuned in this fashion the integrity of the Pythagorean tuning would thereby be preserved.

4 The Greater Perfect System

Once established, the Dorian scale system came to occupy the same niche in classical Greek music, as the C major scale does for Western musicians today, that is as a kind of default scale. Directly comparable with the modern C major scale, it was probably the first scale system that a young lyre player would learn to play. Furthermore, as scholar of ancient Greek music Stefan Hagel points out, it was the scale most esteemed by Plato and Aristotle.[19]

The genera...

Yet the Dorian represented but one scale amongst a great variety of musical scales and modes recognized by ancient Greek musicians. One method of classifying these scales was according to their *genus*, which was determined by the type of tetrachords that they used. There were three basic *genera*: the *diatonic*, *chromatic* and *enharmonic*. Scale systems could belong to any one of these three genera or a combination.

With so many different scales and modes being used, it is not surprising that at some point, attempts were made to bring some kind of order to the ancient Greek scale system. One of the

---

[19] Ibid., p. 9.

steps taken towards this end was the recognition of an expanded pitch array, first elucidated in the work *Sections of a Canon* (around 400 BC) formerly attributed to Euclid. Called the *Greater Perfect System*, this expanded pitch array possessed a span of a double octave and embraced some fifteen separate scale degrees.

Extension of the Dorian system...

The Greater Perfect System consisted of a basic Dorian scale, which occupied the middle of the system, at either extreme of which were added two conjunct tetrachords. These were the hyperbolaîon tetrachord, which ended with nétē, and the hýpaton tetrachord, which descended from hypátē. See fig. 4.1.

Fig. 4.1: Hýpaton and Hyperbolaîon Tetrachords

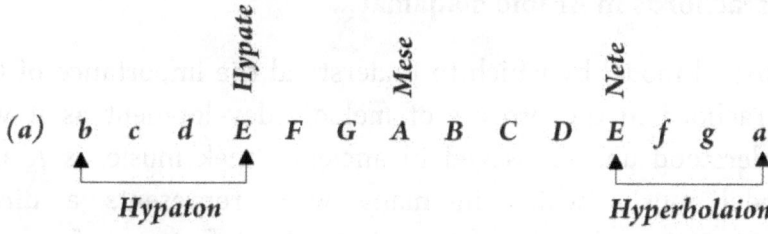

A final foundation note called proslambanómenos (meaning added-on) was then added to complete a double-octave compass. The reason for this addition was probably more for the purposes of giving the system a sense of balance, than any purely practical musical reasons. Ancient Greek musicians conceived of mésē as lying at the very centre point of the musical cosmos. Without proslambanómenos, mésē is slightly off centre – one of the perceived defects perhaps, of the original Dorian scale.

As far as modern musicians are concerned, there is no problem recognizing the Greater Perfect System as a two-octave range of the white keys stretching from A_2 to A_4 on the keyboard. Moreover, they would be quite right in that recognition. However, ascribing proslambanómenos the pitch of note A is simply a matter of convenience so that the Greater Perfect System can be represented using Western methods of notation.

Although the range of notes used might be familiar to modern musicians, the strong emphasis that the Greater Perfect system places upon the tetrachord is not at all familiar today. Musicians of antiquity thought of scale systems, not in terms of closed octaves, but as growing chains of connected tetrachords, linked together either conjunctly, through the sharing of a common tone, or disjunctly, through media of a tone of disjunction. Each such tetrachord clearly represented a specific zone or area of focus for melodic activity.

Tetrachords in Arabic maqamat...

A useful model by which to understand the importance of the tetrachord in the process of melodic development as it was understood and envisaged in ancient Greek music, is Arabic modal music, which in many ways represents a direct continuation of some of the most salient features of ancient Greek musical traditions. This process of continuation was largely enabled by the translation into Arabic of a great number of ancient Greek works, including works on music. No doubt inspired by these translations, numerous theoretical treatises on music were written in Arabic, by authors such as Al Kindi (810 – 873), whose treatment of the subject involved the introduction of an entire roster of correspondences between music and the cosmos, based on Pythagorean numerology.

One of the most comprehensive treatises produced during this era was the *Kitab-al-Musiqa al-Kabir* by Al Farabi (872-950). This treatise established the grounds for a precise scientific approach to the subject of music, one that dealt with practical topics such as the nature of sound, the construction and derivation of musical instruments, the nature of tone, intervals, *different* types of tetrachords and musical modes.

Al Farabi also dealt with the subject of tuning, in particular the placing of frets upon the lute in such a way as to be enable the playing of those neutral intervals, those which figured prominently in various modal shades as mentioned by Aristoxenus and Ptolemy.[20] For those interested in this subject generally, one of the most comprehensive sources written in the English language is Scott Marcus' thesis *Arab Music Theory in the Modern Period* (1990), which at over 800 pages, represents a fabulous compendium of very accessible information upon the subject.

Ajnas...

An important feature of Arabic modal music is the use of a distinctive set of modal forms, particular frameworks for melodic improvisation comparable in a sense to Hindu rãgs, these being called *maqamat*. The scalar building blocks for maqamat, *ajnas* (or *jins* in the singular), are groups of three to five adjacent notes of the mode that denote a particular zone or region of self-contained melodic activity. Zones of three notes are called trichords; four notes tetrachords and five notes pentachords. These are illustrated in fig. 4.2.

Arabic modal melodies tend to develop within these clearly defined melodic zones, bounded as they are by notes that tend to bear a consonant relationship to one another. This gives to the melodies a sense of organization, stability and structure, as well as imparting to certain notes a pronounced functional

---

[20] See chapters 7 and 8.

importance.

Fig. 4.2: *Three Types of Ajnas*

```
Trichord    A  B  c  d  E  f  g  A
            ↑     ↑
            └─────┘

Tetrachord  A  B  c  d  E  f  g  A
            ↑        ↑
            └────────┘

Pentachord  A  B  c  d  E  f  g  A
            ↑           ↑
            └───────────┘
```

Modal tonic and dominant...

The lowest note of the jins for example, provides a firm anchor for the melody. Functionally speaking, it may therefore be described as being the *modal tonic*. As the melody rises up from the tonic, it finds the lower note of the upper jins, which, bearing a consonant relationship to the tonic offers a natural resting place for the melody. Functionally speaking this note may therefore be described as being the *modal dominant*.

Fig. 4.3: *Melodic Movement between Modal Tonic and Dominant*

From that melodically dominant note, the direction of melodic motion can often reverse in which case the modal melody can head back down towards the tonic as shown in fig 4.3a). Alternatively, the modal dominant can provide the platform and impetus for melodic motion that heads further upwards. Eventually it then meets a note that, having a fundamental consonant relationship to the tonic of 2/1, offers another natural resting point, as shown in fig. 4.3b. This note is the octave of the modal tonic (ratio 2/1).

Forming a natural frame or boundary for the development of the melody, the direction of the melody can then reverse and head back towards the modal dominant. In this way the modal dominant serves as a junction point which both connects and separates the two main areas of a melody, the lower jins bounded by the modal tonic and dominant and the upper jins bounded by the modal dominant and the octave of the modal tonic (fig. 4.4)

Fig. 4.4: *The Lower and Upper Jins*

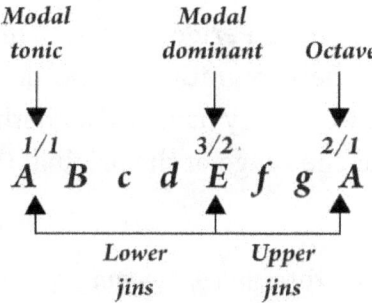

Having reached the octave, the melody might then develop sufficient impetus to explore the lower jins as it repeats itself in the octave above, in which case a basic extension of the scale is needed above the modal tonic (fig. 4.5).

Fig. 4.5: *Upper Extension of the Octave Scale*

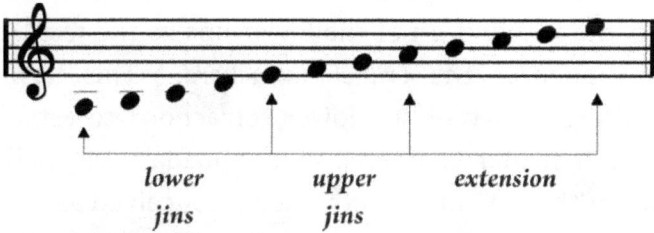

Similarly, when the melody eventually heads back down towards the tonic, it may go below the tonic and meet the upper jins in the octave below. The note just beneath the tonic finds great importance here, as a natural leading note back up to the tonic. To accommodate this process, another extension of the scale is needed, to result in an overall scale of two octaves, which contains four tetrachords (fig. 4.6).

The Arabic double octave...

Therefore, although maqam are often represented within a one-octave range, a fuller exposition of the possibilities of a maqam can be more effectively realized over a more extensive two-octave range. One of the interesting features of this is that the double-octave expression of the maqam is very reminiscent of the ancient Greek Greater Perfect System. This in its turn might even suggest that the recognition of the need for melodies to develop in certain ways, may have had something to do with the felt need to extend the range of the original Dorian scale to two octaves.

Fig. 4.6: *Two Octave Expression of Maqam*

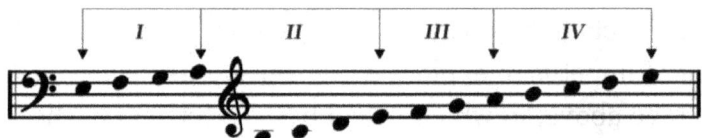

Root and branch tetrachords...

One of the uniquely original features of Arabic modal music theory is the recognition of the lower jins as the *root tetrachord* and the upper as the *branch tetrachord*.[21] This terminology reflects the capacity of the lower tetrachord to establish the fundamental modal character of the maqam, as well as the observation that the upper tetrachord, conceived as the branch

---

[21] Scott Marcus (1989), *Arabic Music Theory in the Modern Period*, p. 315.

of the more fundamental root, serves to contribute additional colour to the mode.

Clearly, this concept applies to more than just Arabic modal music. For Western musicians can easily relate this observation to the various forms of the minor mode. These all share in the same *root* tetrachord, which gives to different types of minor mode their primary and most recognizable characteristic. Consequently, variations in the minor mode only occur with respect to the *branch* tetrachord, which in the natural minor mode is E F G A, in the harmonic minor mode E F G# A and in the melodic minor mode (ascending) E F# G#A. As branch tetrachords, they therefore add a new colour into the mix.

Proof of the tremendous influence of the root tetrachord lies in the observation that the latter – the melodic minor mode – is only one note different to the major mode in its entirety. Yet this one note, as it appears in the root tetrachord, colours the entire mode with an undoubtedly minor character.

Features of the Greater Perfect System...

In the absence of a considerable body of ancient Greek music to study, a brief consideration of Arabic maqamat at least provides a sense of the priorities at play when the tetrachord is established as the basic unit of melodic organization. In Greece it seems that these tetrachords could be added above one another, below one another, either conjunctly or disjunctly – with a tone of disjunction separating them. An octave scale was therefore conceived as being a composite structure containing three interlinked elements – an upper and a lower tetrachord and a tone of disjunction. These could also be arranged in various ways with respect to one another; with the tone of disjunction between the tetrachords, in the case of regular modes, above two conjunct tetrachords, in the case of 'Hyper' modes and below two conjunct tetrachords in the case of 'Hypo' modes.

Fig. 4.7: *The Greater Perfect System*

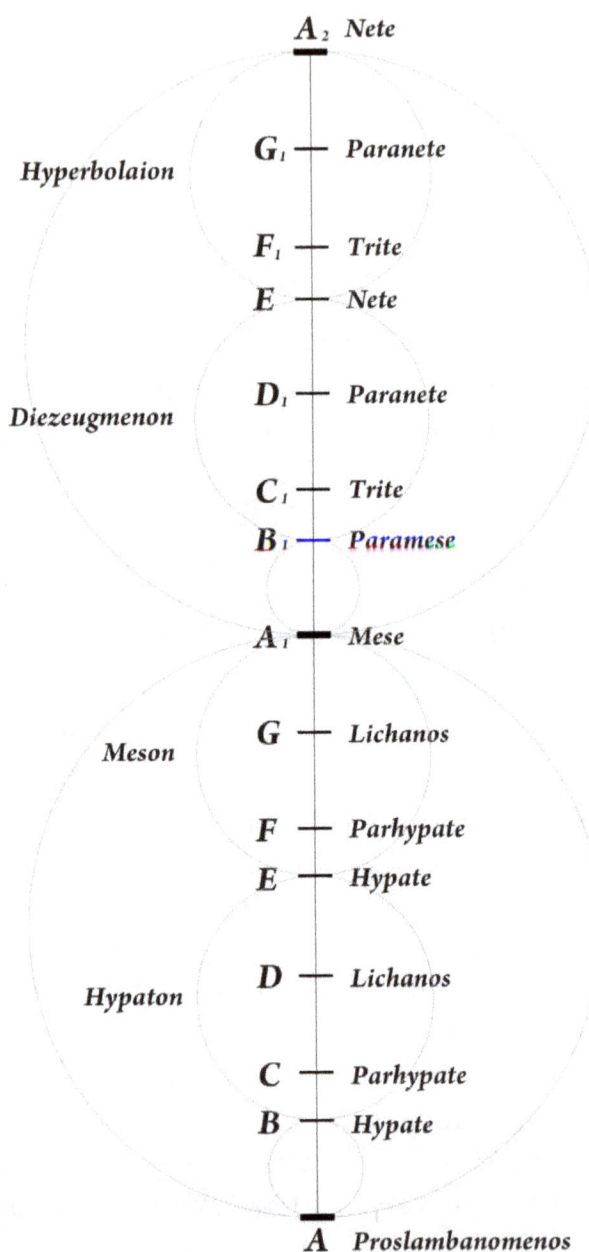

The Greater Perfect System, was consequently thought of, not as being a two-octave scale, but as a connected chain of four tetrachords linked by two tones of disjunction. Indeed, a closer inspection of the Greater Perfect System reveals that:

- The foundation tone proslambanómenos was separated from the hýpaton tetrachord by *a tone of disjunction*.
- The highest note of the hýpaton tetrachord was at the same time the lowest note of the méson tetrachord whose upper note was the mésē. They were therefore conjunct, as opposed to disjunct tetrachords.
- Separating the méson tetrachord from the tetrachord above, referred to as diezeugménon, was a tone of disjunction between mésē and paramésē. The méson and diezeugménon are thereby related as disjunct tetrachords.
- The upper note of the diezeugménon tetrachord was at the same time the lower note of the hyperbolaîon tetrachord that capped and completed the double octave system. Diezeugménon and hyperbolaîon were thus related as conjunct tetrachords.

These features may be scrutinized through reference to an illustration of the Greater Perfect System provided for in fig. 4.7. The names ascribed to the four tetrachords reflect their position within the Greater Perfect System as a whole. Hýpaton signified the farthest tetrachord, while méson signified the middle tetrachord. The term diezeugménon in its turn, reflected the fact that this tetrachord began on paramésē i.e. the note immediately above the mésē that acted as the tone of disjunction (*dieuxis*). The names given to these tetrachords also enabled each note of the Greater Perfect System to be individually named. In this way, it became possible to distinguish between say hypátē hýpaton and hypátē méson. The former referred to hypátē in the hýpaton tetrachord, while the latter referred to hypátē in the méson tetrachord.

Mathematically speaking, the Greater Perfect System showed a certain logic that related it to earlier models of the musical scale. Much of this logic is evidently geometric in its sensibility. Observe for example in fig. 4.8, how the double octave range of the Greater Perfect System does not exceed the bounds of the Pythagorean Tetractys.

Fig. 4.8: *The Greater Perfect System and the Tetractys*

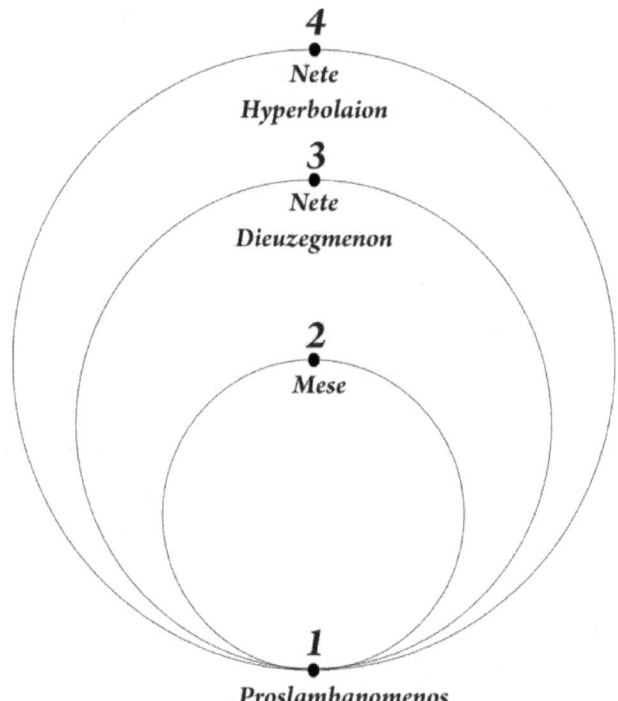

The ratio of nétē to nétē diezeugménon is thus 4:3, etc.. It is notable that within this defining framework, the fixed tones are all related by a series of simple ratios that enable their expression by a series of fundamental whole numbers that extends from eighth to thirty-two, a series that imparts to the Greater Perfect System a distinct sense of architectural strength and integrity. See fig. 4.9 for an illustration of this.

Fig. 4.9: *The Fixed Tones of the Greater Perfect System*

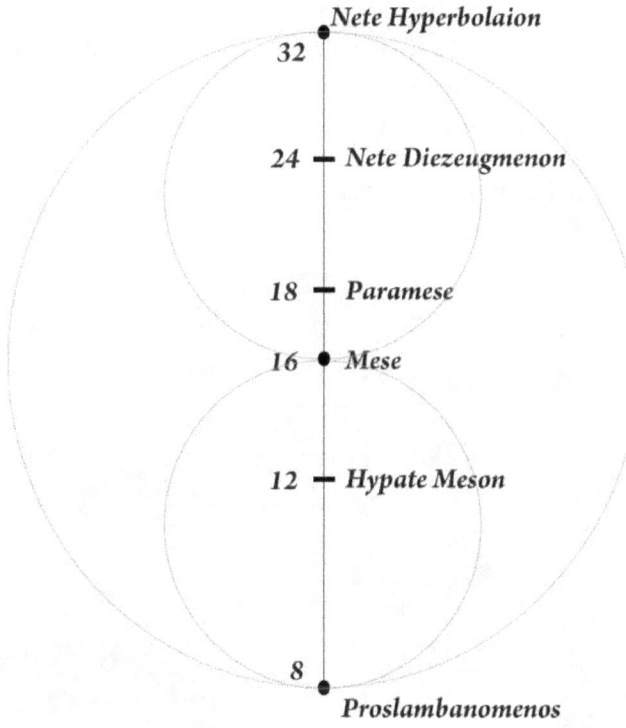

The Lesser Perfect System...

Alongside the Great Perfect system there was the Lesser Perfect System. This ostensibly appeared as a downward extension of the antique heptachord of Terpander, consisting of three tetrachords, one of which was unique to the lesser perfect system - the synēmménōn tetrachord stretching down from nétē to mésē.

The most conspicuous feature of the Lesser Perfect System, is that, unlike the Greater Perfect which is a disjunct system, the

Lesser Perfect is a *conjunct system*, composed as it is, from three conjunct tetrachords spanning a range of some eleven notes. Another conspicuous feature, which becomes readily evident when the Lesser Perfect System is represented by Western note values, is the appearance of note B flat in the synēmménōn tetrachord, which seems to be in direct conflict with the B natural in the hýpaton tetrachord. This can be appreciated further through reference to the illustration of the Lesser Perfect System in fig. 4.10.

Fig. 4.10: *The Lesser Perfect System*

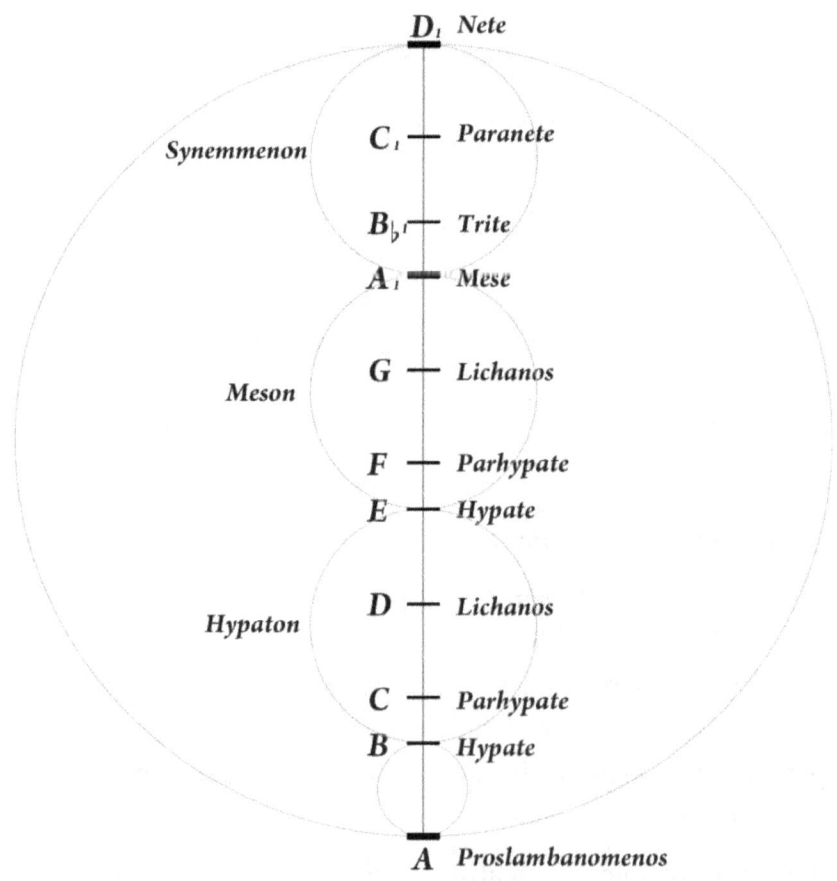

This apparent conflict is explained by the observation that ancient Greek musicians recognized two kinds of scale systems. There were non-modulating scale systems in which, it was assumed, there would be no change of mode during the performance of a composition. The Greater Perfect System therefore counts as such. Then there were modulating scale systems, which assumed a change of mode would take place.

One rational explanation of the potential need for such a system lies in the observation that the strings of a lyre or cithara need to be tuned prior to a performance. It therefore becomes apparent that any changes of mode that might take place during that performance would need to be anticipated during the tuning process. Probably connected with this is the observation that at the general time the system was being formulated, the cithara already had a full complement of eleven strings, which just happens to be the number of notes in the Lesser Perfect System.

The modulatory capabilities of the Lesser Perfect System become apparent when it is seen that the two lower tetrachords, inclusive of proslambanómenos, conform to the original Dorian system, while the two upper tetrachords, inclusive of lichanós hýpaton, imply a Dorian system transposed a fifth lower i.e. another key of the same scale system. Fig. 4.11 illustrates this in which the lower circle represents the original Dorian system, the upper circle its modulated form.

Presumably modulations to a key a fifth below were so common that they needed to be accommodated through the formulation of a modulating system. Therefore the Lesser Perfect System seems to be comparable to the scheme of keys in Western music known as the cycle of fifths, whereby closely related keys i.e. keys whose tonic lies a fifth up or a fifth down from each other are represented as being adjacent to one another. In this case, the Lesser Perfect System appears as a single link in a chain that ultimately connected all of the various keys used together.

Fig. 4.11: *The Lesser Perfect as Modulating System*

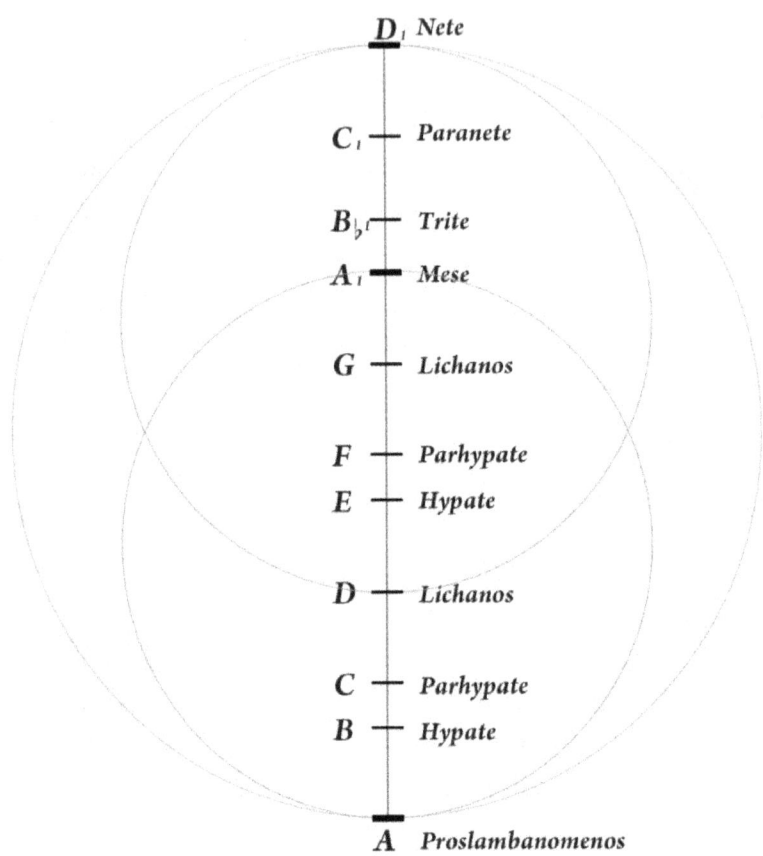

The perfect or immutable system...

When combined together the Greater and Lesser Perfect Systems then gave rise to the *Perfect or Immutable System*. In diagrammatic representations of this system the synēmmḗnōn tetrachord tends to have been portrayed either as being nestled in between the diezeugménon and meson tetrachords, or else standing alongside them (see fig. 4.12).

This system represents the backdrop against which can be

understood and placed all of the various musical scales and modes used by ancient Greek musicians. Once grasped and understood it then becomes possible to proceed with a more in depth study of individual scales.

Fig. 4.12: *The Perfect or Immutable System*

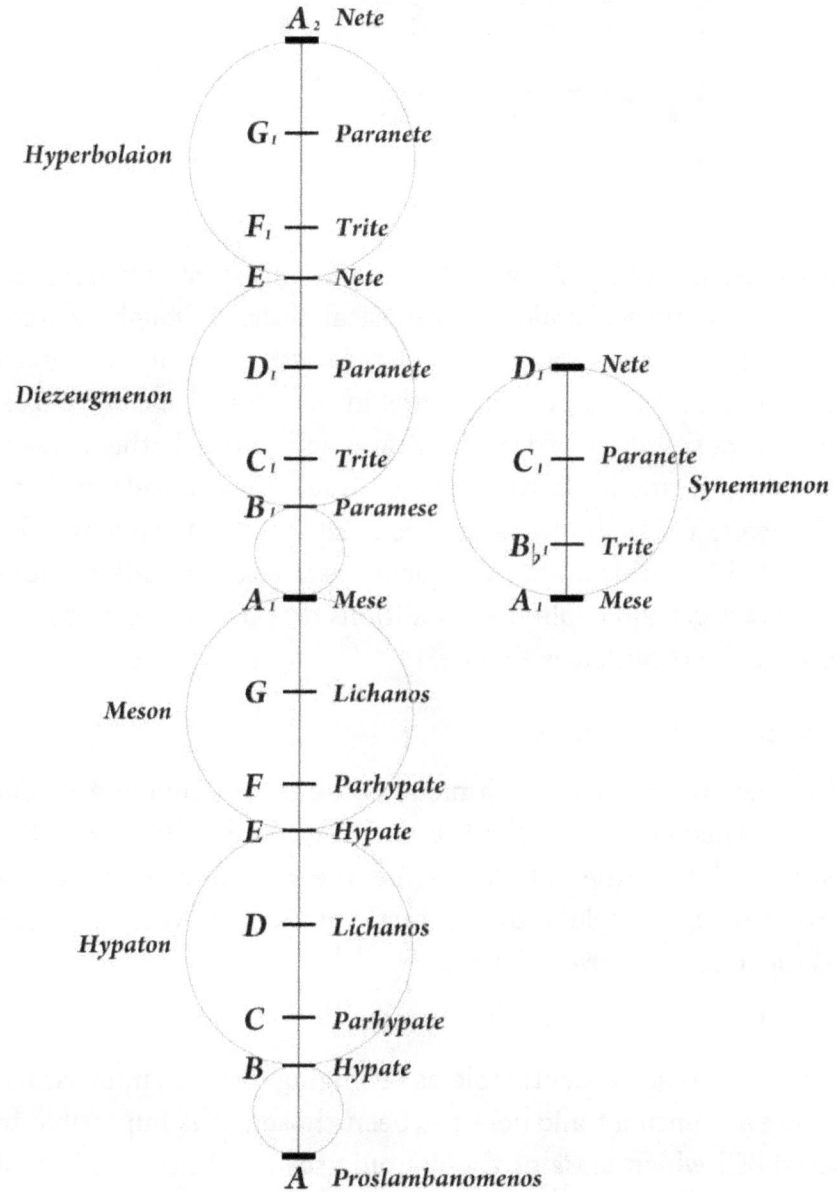

5 The Seven Harmoniai

No musician could deny that there is an essential difference between a musical *scale* and a musical *mode*. Although related, the former tends to be associated with a group of notes arranged in their ascending, or as in the case of ancient Greek music, descending order of progression through the octave. Such for example, is the ancient Greek Dorian scale system. However, although identifiable as being a *scale*, it cannot yet be asserted that this scale may qualify as a *mode*. This is because there are certain qualifying conditions that need to be met for a scale to be regarded as a mode.

The modal tonic note...

The first pre-requisite of a mode is the recognition of a modal tonic. This will enable the listener to gauge which note of the scale counts as the note of rest i.e. the first note of the series. An obvious example of this, in terms of modern Western music, is the following series of notes:

    A   B   C   D   E   F   G   A   B   C   D   E   Etc.

These are readily identifiable as belonging to the diatonic scale. However, until a tonic note has been chosen, it is impossible to establish which *mode* of the diatonic scale is being implied. If note A is chosen to be the tonic, then it is clear that the above series of notes refer to a two octave range of the A natural minor scale. However, if note C is chosen to be the tonic, it is clear that the range of notes presented above belong to the mode of C major.

Now as the tonic note is chosen, this means that *mode* is a psychological phenomenon created by the listener's recognition and perception of *modal functions*. The primary modal function is therefore the tonic, which not only establishes the beginning or first step of the note series, but also represents the central point of reference for the melody, against which and in relation to which, all other notes of the scale will be heard and compared. In this way, the other notes of the scale then acquire their own functions within the mode as a whole.

Modal functions...

Because of this, the same note can perform different modal functions depending upon the context in which it is used. Therefore, relative to note A as modal tonic, note C forms a minor third relationship with it, while relative to note G as modal tonic, the same note C forms a perfect fourth relationship with the tonic note. Minor third and perfect fourth in this instance, are terms of expression that carry a certain amount of information about these vital modal functions.

Understanding that modality depends upon the establishment of these note functions, the important question to ask therefore, is did ancient Greek musicians recognize a modal tonic or indeed, any other kind of modal function. If the answer lies in the affirmative, then it is possible to conclude that ancient Greek music was essentially modal in its primary vectors of expression. Now examining the evidence that is available, it becomes apparent that ancient Greek musicians *did* recognize one particular note as being more important than others are. This note was the mésē, the central tone of the Greater Perfect System.

The mésē as modal tonic…

In his *Problems* Aristotle observed that: "All good melodies often employ the tone of the middle string, and good composers often come upon it, and if they leave it recur to it again; but this is not the case with any other tone…."[22] He later states "in this way the tone of the middle string is a link between tones, especially of the best tones, because its tone most frequently recurs".[23]

Cleonides also writes about the importance of the mésē, observing, "It is from the mésē that the functions of the remaining notes are recognized, for how each of them functions becomes apparent in relation to the mésē."[24] In this statement, Cleonides summarizes the role of the modal tonic with absolute precision, a role that is responsible for imparting a modal function to all of the other notes. Moreover, these functions he correctly observes, derive from the relationship of those notes to the modal tonic – the mésē.

Other statements he makes tend to confirm this, although the language does become rather obtuse as he struggles to explain his meaning: "Function is the order of the note in the scale; or, function is the order of the note, through which we recognize each of the notes."[25] As can be seen, Cleonides knows what he

---

[22] Aristotle, *Problems*, xix.20

[23] Ibid, xix36.

[24] Mathiesen, *Op. Cit*, p.383.

[25] *Ibid.*, p. 384.

wants to say, but struggles in the process of doing so, clearly lacking the precise language and descriptive terminology needed to explain the basis for vital modal functions.

The importance given to the mésē as modal tonic is reflected in that branch of musical philsophy that saw in the musical scale systems of antiquity a direct expression and reflection of the cosmic order, as it was seen to manifest through the septenary of the planets of the solar system – inclusive of the heavenly bodies of the sun and moon.

Now while various authorities differed in terms of the precise correspondence between scale tones and planets, they were all in agreement on one point. The mésē found its cosmological reflection in the sphere of the sun, the central sphere around which everything else revolved. See table 4 for a depiction of the correspondence between planets and tones as designated by Nicomachus.

Table 4: *Correspondence of Planets and Tones*

Note	String	Planet
D	Nétē	Moon
C	Paranétē	Venus
Bb	Paramésē	Mercury
A	Mésē	Sun
G	Lichanós	Mars
F	Parhypátē	Jupiter
E	Hypátē	Saturn

The seven harmoniai...

By presuming the mésē to be modal tonic (1/1), the Dorian system can then be recognized as being a melodic mode. Furthermore, given that note A could perform the function of modal tonic, so therefore could any other note of the scale.

Therefore, there are seven *possible* modes of the diatonic scale obtained by ascribing the function of the tonic in each case to a different note of the scale.

At one level these were referred to as *harmoniai* and were named after other ancient Greek tribes whose temperaments were felt to be similar to the particular moods or feel of the harmoniai so obtained. The names that were given to the seven harmonia, together with their characteristic octave ranges are as shown in table 5:

Table 5: *The Seven Harmonia*

- The *Dorian harmonia*:   E F G A B C D E
- the *Phrygian harmonia*:   D E F G A B C D
- the *Lydian harmonia*:   C D E F G A B C
- the *Mixolydian harmonia*:   B C D E F G A B
- the *Hypodorian harmonia*:   A B C D E F G A
- the *Hypophrygian harmonia*:   G A B C D E F G
- the *Hypolydian harmonia*:   F G A B C D E F

The seven octave species...

One of the chief accommodating features of the Greater Perfect System is that it embraced all seven of these harmoniai and their particular octave ranges. These are shown in relation to the Greater Perfect System as a whole in fig. 5.1. The only note that was not needed for this process was Proslambanomenos, the foundation tone of the system, which was probably added for no other reason than to preserve the position of the mésē as lying at the very heart and centre of the Greater Perfect System.

Ancient Greek theorists also observed that each mode could be uniquely identified by the particular sequence of magnitudes arising from the sizes of the scale steps, these being of two kinds – tones and semitones. Each such sequence was referred to as a particular *octave species* and identified with the harmoniai whose scale step pattern was so indicated.

Fig. 5.1: *The Greater Perfect System and the Seven Harmoniai*

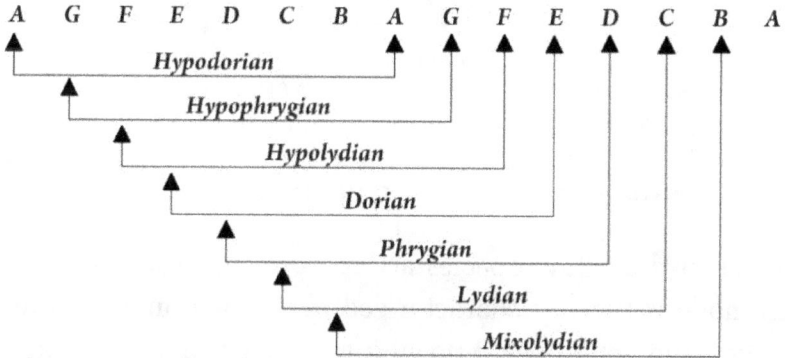

These species can be appreciated further by representing the octave as a circle, and the notes of the scale as points on the perimeter of the circle. Each of the seven octave species traces a complete cycle around the octave which, beginning at a different position, gives rise to a different sequential order of intervals. In the illustration of this provided for in fig. 5.2 a whole tone is represented by the number 2, a limma by the number 1.

Fig. 5.2 shows that the sequence of interval magnitudes for the Dorian octave species is 2 2 1 2 2 2 1, while the sequence for the Hypolydian is 1 2 2 1 2 2 2, etc. A representation of these octave species as associated with the seven harmoniai can be seen in table 6. The magnitudes of the scale steps are presented in their descending order through the octave.

Fig. 5.2: *Order of Intervals Within Each of the Seven Harmoniai*

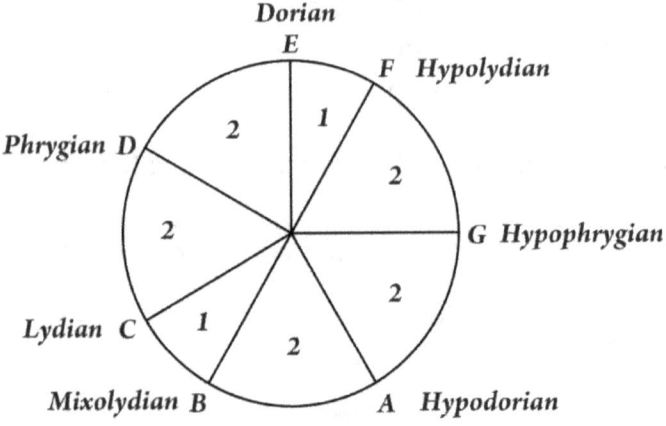

Interest in the octave species arises from the observation that each mode is thereby characterized by its own unique pattern of tones and semitones. Knowing this, it becomes possible to understand, at least in part, how the ear becomes capable of recognizing these modes when heard. This is because of their melodic tendencies as determined and reflected by that particular species. Obvious examples of this are say, the prominent semitone step between the first and second degree of the Dorian mode, or the whole tone step between the seventh and the octave of the modal tonic in modes such as the Hypophrygian. In the Lydian mode, this step is only a semitone.

However, the essence of modal expression lies in the vital modal functions generated by the presence of the modal tonic. If it were not for this vital principle, the ear would not be capable of recognizing which note of the original scale was functioning as the melodic reference point. Without this capability, the mode's unique identifying pattern would therefore be useless.

Table 6: *Modes and Octave Species*

Mode							
Dorian:	2	2	1	2	2	2	1
Phrygian:	2	1	2	2	2	1	2
Lydian:	1	2	2	2	1	2	2
Mixolydian:	2	2	2	1	2	2	1
Hypodorian:	2	2	1	2	2	1	2
Hypophrygian:	2	1	2	2	1	2	2
Hypolydian:	1	2	2	1	2	2	2

The diatonic modes of Babylonian music...

For the modern musician, the scheme of seven modes just shown no doubt puts them on very familiar ground. Indeed, despite obvious differences in the ancient Greek names that are used today (passed on through an inherited error of nomenclature by the early Christian church), it is evident that the seven harmoniai are identical in substance with the seven modes of the diatonic scale. Consequently, when composers and musicians use these modes, although their use might be significantly different to that of antiquity, nonetheless this system of seven modes, or in ancient Greek terms seven *harmoniai*, clearly has a long history behind it.

The question is, how far back in history the recognition and usage of these seven modes does go. In terms of ancient Greek music, there is unfortunately insufficient evidence to establish this. However, there is evidence to show that much earlier cultures used this system of modes, which might in its turn indicate that the seven harmoniai of ancient Greek music may ultimately have originated with those cultures.

Signs of the usage of advanced scale systems prior to their use in ancient Greek music, appeared with the discovery of the golden lyre that was excavated from the ancient Sumerian Royal Tomb of Ur that dates back to about 2,500 years BC – meaning that it predated even the erection of Stonehenge or the building of the Great Pyramid. This lyre was royally decorated with a golden bulls head, gold and silver sheeting and some five thousand separate pieces of cut precious stone. Unfortunately, the lyre was mostly destroyed along with other priceless artefacts during an unfortunate and relatively recent looting of the Baghdad Museum.[26] The gold and silver sheeting had been unceremoniously torn off and the violently severed bull's head was later recovered from the vault of a local bank.

Within the original Tomb of Ur some sixty bodies were found, whose deaths were possibly due to a mass suicide. One such body was evidently of a harpist, the position of whose instrument as found during excavations, suggests that she was probably singing right up until the moment of her untimely death, possibly due to taking a slow acting poison.

For mythologist Joseph Campbell the golden bull's head suggested the song of the moon-bull, composed in imitation of the music of the spheres, that harmonious hum of the cosmos which found its echo in the internal harmony of the human soul. This idea, he pointed out, is one intrinsic to Confucian and Indian music as well as to "the continuous chanting of the monks, who were diligently practicing in accord with the choir of the angels".[27] It was also intrinsic to ancient Greek music, whose sounds were similarly envisaged to represent but a crude imitation of the ethereal harmony of the spheres.

---

[26] Read about the heartening tale of a reconstruction of the Golden Lyre of Ur at this web address: http://www.lyre-of-ur.com/history.htm

[27] Joseph Campbell, *Oriental Mythology*, p.114.

Ancient evidence for the seven modes ...

Although the construction of instruments such as the golden lyre of Ur undoubtedly suggests the use of equally advanced musical scales, evidence uncovered comparatively recently by scholars such as Anne Kilmer and Marcelle Duchesne-Guillemin, who managed to decipher a series of musical writings and notations inscribed on clay tablets dating from the second millennium BC, confirmed this pretty conclusively.

These clay tablets show that Babylonian music used a seven note diatonic scale and that seven modes or heptachords were derived from it, all seven of which were recognized and named. These were not only tuned methodically, but connected with the method of tuning was an ingenious system for passing from one mode to another.[28]

The method of tuning used was the fifth up/fourth down or fourth up/fifth down method, already mentioned as the basic method for tuning the ancient Greek lyre (Pythagorean tuning). The method of passing from one mode to another was connected with one of the strange anomalies of the tonal world, where one particular link in the chain of fifths/fourths will always be discordant.

In the case of the cycle of fourths, the discordant link is provided for by the diminished fifth, while in the case of the cycle of fifths, the augmented fourth performs the same role. This is the so-called *devils fourth* of the Middle Ages which, interrupting the otherwise serene and stately procession of fourths and fifths, proved so troublesome to the monastic theorists of Medieval Western music.

---

[28] Marcelle Duchesne-Guillemin's *A Hurrian Musical Score from Ugarit: The Discovery of Mesopotamian Music*, Sources from the Ancient Near East, Vol. 2 Fascicle 2, pp. 5 – 26.

This awkward sounding discord occurs after the sixth cycle, thereby representing the end of the sequence of fifths that gives rise to the seven note diatonic scale. Beyond this point lies the chromatic world of sharps and flats. Accordingly, the seventh fifth (starting from note F) produces note F sharp, while the seventh fourth (starting from note B) produces note B flat. As such the point in the sequence where the 'devil's fourth' appears represents that demarcation point between one musical domain and another: the diatonic and the chromatic.

The cyclic method of tuning, already discussed with reference to tuning the ancient Greek lyre, is illustrated in fig. 5.3, which shows the Babylonian mode *Nis Gabari*, as transcribed into Western notation and tuned using this method.

Fig. 5.3: *Cyclic Tuning of Nis Gabari*

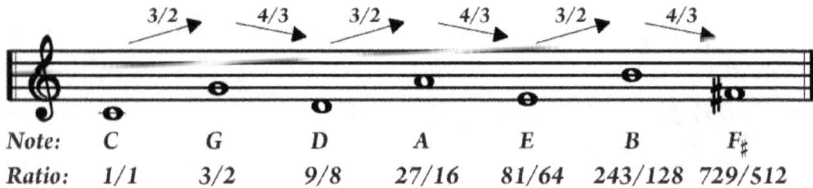

Note:	C	G	D	A	E	B	F♯
Ratio:	1/1	3/2	9/8	27/16	81/64	243/128	729/512

Observe that the augmented fourth is reached very last in the chain of fifths/fourths, meaning that it is the note most distantly related to the starting note, a relationship reflected in the complexity of the ratio which is 729/512. The difference between the aural quality of a perfect fifth and an augmented fourth is considerable, which means that whatever mode is being tuned, the string that produces the augmented fourth or diminished fifth is therefore best left until last. This is because of the sheer difficulty of tuning this interval by ear when compared with the ease of tuning a perfect fifth or fourth.

The tuning up and down principle...

Another interesting discovery was that a tuning up or down method was used in order to be able to change from one mode to another.[29] This was based on the principle of eliminating the discordant augmented fourth or diminished fifth in a mode, and in the process of doing so, change from one mode to another. In the case of the Babylonian mode *Nis Gabris*, this occurred with respect to the fourth degree. Using the tuning down principle observe that note F# can be lowered by a semitone to produce note F as shown in fig. 5.4:

Fig. 5.4: *Eliminating Augmented Fourth by Tuning Down Principle*

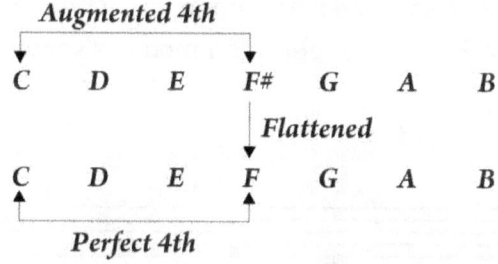

This then produces a new heptatonic mode *Nid Qablim* corresponding to the ancient Greek Lydian mode (fig. 5.5).

Fig. 5.5: *Nid Qablim*

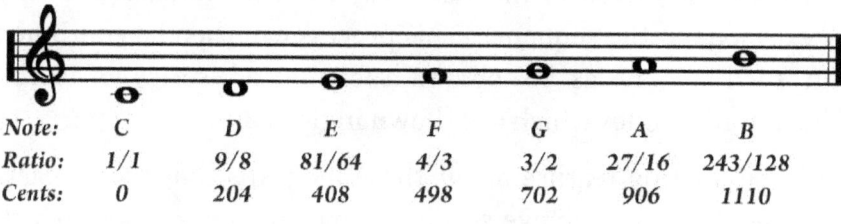

Note:	C	D	E	F	G	A	B
Ratio:	1/1	9/8	81/64	4/3	3/2	27/16	243/128
Cents:	0	204	408	498	702	906	1110

---

[29] Ibid.

In Nid Qablim there is an augmented fourth between notes F and B. To arrive at the next mode in the sequence, this was eliminated by flattening the B as shown in fig.5.6:

Fig. 5.6: *Eliminating Augmented Fourth by Tuning Down Principle*

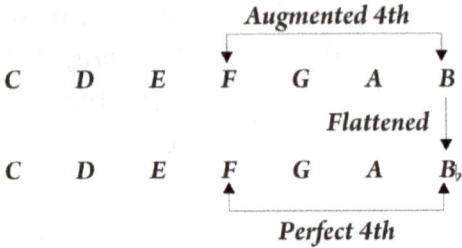

This then gives rise to another mode *Pitum*, which is equivalent to the ancient Greek Hypophrygian mode as shown in fig. 5.7.

Fig. 5.7: *Pitum*

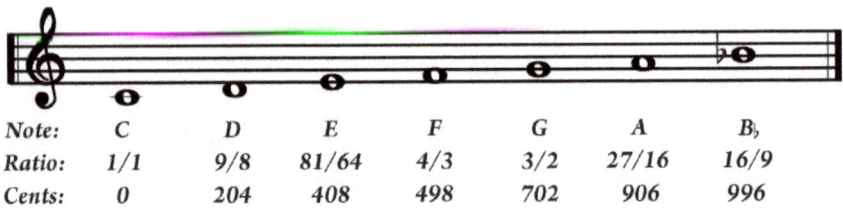

Note:	C	D	E	F	G	A	B♭
Ratio:	1/1	9/8	81/64	4/3	3/2	27/16	16/9
Cents:	0	204	408	498	702	906	996

In this new mode the augmented fourth/diminished fifth can then be eliminated in the same way in order to change to the next mode in the sequence. This process can then be continued in such a way as to obtain a connected series of seven heptatonic modes which are shown in fig. 5.8.

The fascinating feature about these modes is that they clearly parallel the seven octave species of ancient Greek music, which in their turn, bear a direct relationship to the seven diatonic modes used by modern Western musicians. This indicates that certain long term enduring musical values, as reflected in a general preference for the use of diatonic scales, may ultimately have its roots in the music of ancient Babylon. Their melodies therefore, would have probably sounded very familiar.

Fig. 5.8: *Sequence of Heptatonic Modes*

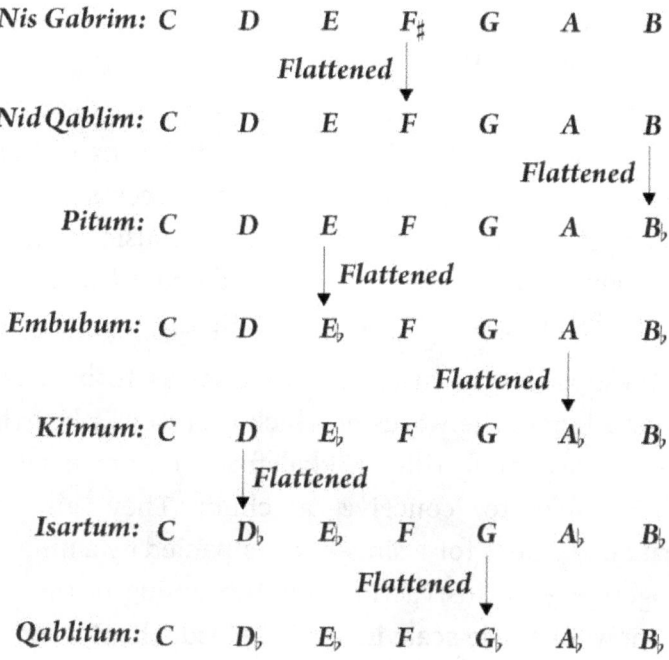

Although for the purposes of this section, the results of this extraordinary research have been simplified and presented in accessible terms, there are still numerous cloudy areas, which might yet lead to some radically different conclusions. There is some confusion about the direction of the scale: was it conceived as a rising heptachordal scale, as in the West, or a falling heptachordal scale, as in the heptachord of Terpander?[30] Depending on how the scale is interpreted – rising or falling – the modes will therefore bear different names. Yet this is essentially an issue of nomenclature, rather than one of

---

[30] For a discussion of the issues involved, see Leon Crickmore, *New Light on the Babylonian Tonal System*, ICONEA, 2008, pp. 11 – 22.

principle. Furthermore, because it is not clear if any functions were assigned to the notes of a particular heptachord, it is difficult to make a more specific comparison with the ancient Greek modes.

The oldest song in the world…

In recent years, considerable interest has been shown in what has sometimes been described as the oldest song of the world. This song became known through the successful efforts of Assyriologist Anne Kilmer to decipher musical inscriptions found upon a series of clay tablets dated to about 1400BC, excavated from the site of the ancient Ugarit.

Upon these tablets is inscribed what seems to be a complete score for a hymn, the words of which represent a heartfelt plea to the Goddess of fertility Nikkal from a women who found herself unable to conceive a child. They also contain performance guides for a singer accompanied by a nine stringed lyre together with instructions for the tuning of the lyre. The latter shows that the scale in use is indeed a heptatonic scale of the diatonic type.

Numerous attempts have been made to transcribe this hymn into Western notation and perform it as originally intended. Anne Kilmer's transcription is particularly interesting, as it seems to imply that the song used two-part harmony featuring consonant thirds and sixths.[31] As these are appreciably 'sweetened' through use of harmonic thirds and sixths, rather than the thirds and sixths generated by cyclic methods of tuning, this interpretation of the song engendered a certain amount of criticism from some Western academics, who believe

---

[31] Precise details together with Midi files of Ann Kilmer's interpretation of the song can be found here: http://www.amaranthpublishing.com/hurrian.htm

that harmony using consonant thirds and sixths, was only developed in the West during the Middle Ages.

Attempts have also been made to arrange this song into a format where it could be played by Western instruments. Recently I heard a version performed by the Russian Symphony Orchestra arranged and composed by the Syrian composer Malek Jandali (b. 1972). However, as his arrangement used techniques of harmony and counterpoint reminiscent of Western music of the nineteenth century, it was clear that his realization of the song from Ugarit was more of an original composition inspired by the melody of the original song.

Another area of interest catalysed by the discovery of these ancient modes of Babylonian music is their potential use in the process of free composition. American composer Lou Harrison (1917 – 2003), who in his lifetime became well known for producing music that used both pure and exotic forms of ancient tuning modes, wrote a *Serenade for Guitar and Percussion* that includes music written in the Babylonian *Isartum* mode. Calling for the use of a guitar with specially adjusted frets which allows this scale to be played with the original tuning, Lou's music has a powerful archaic sense that gives the music an atmosphere of great expressive dignity. This is probably because Lou kept to the original tuning and produced his music in a very authentic sounding melodic style. Lou also recorded a talk on the tuning of the Babylonian harp, which informatively covers some of the topics just considered.[32]

Pertinent questions...

The discovery of an ancient Babylonian scale system, together with a certain type of tuning appropriate for that system, raises

---

[32] Go to http://www.archive.org/details/AM_1971_02_12

a number of questions. One question concerns the origin of this tuning. Today this tuning system is called *Pythagorean tuning* after the figure with whom it tends to be associated. Not using any prime number higher than three, the numbers of the ratios of the crucial intervals involved in the process of Pythagorean tuning – the octave (2/1), perfect fifth (3/2) and perfect fourth (4/3) - all occur within the numerical boundaries of the numbers 1 through to 4, the numbers of the Tetractys already discussed. However, now it appears that Pythagoras might have learned this method of tuning while on his travels to this region of the world. In which case, it would perhaps be more appropriate to refer to Pythagorean tuning as *Babylonian tuning*.

Some scholars of the subject however, have posited the idea that some kind of just intonation might have been used in Babylonian music.[33] This is based on the observation that the numbers associated with certain divinities imply harmonic relationships. Therefore, the number associated with the Babylonian God *Anu* for example is 60, while the number associated with *Sin* is 30. If interpreted as string lengths then it becomes evident that the relationship between Anu and Sin is an octave of ratio 2/1. Similarly, the number associated with *Enlil* is 50 while the number associated with *Ea* is 40. Again, interpreted as string lengths these numbers would imply a harmonic major third relationship of 5/4. If this reasonable theory is correct, then it is feasible that harmonious thirds and sixths might indeed have been both recognized and used, which in turn would go to support Anne Kilmer's transcription of the

---

[33] See Richard Dumbrill's *Goetterzahlen and Scale Structure; The Uruk Lute: Elements of Metrology; The Morphology of the Babylonian Scale*; http://sas.academia.edu/RichardDumbrill/

Ugarit song already discussed - which shows use of thirds and sixths as consonant harmonies in their own right.

Planetary harmonies and the days of the week...

The method of passing from one mode to another is very interesting in the light of ancient Greek conceptions of the cosmos in which the seven planets, by their rotations around the Earth were said to give rise to a planetary heptachord. This has already been mentioned with respect to Nicomachus arrangement in which the longest string of the heptachord corresponds to the most distant and slowest moving sphere of Saturn, the shortest string with the nearest and fastest moving sphere of the moon. However, where did this correlation between the notes of the scale and the seven planets originate? Now if the seven notes in the form of the heptachord originated in Babylon then it is possible that the note - planet system of correspondences also originated in Babylon.

There is an obvious connection with Babylonian architecture here in the form of the seven tiered ziggurat of Borsippa, in which the lowest and largest of the seven tiers was consecrated to the slowest moving sphere Saturn, the highest and smallest to the sphere of the moon. This exactly correlates with Nicomachus scheme of notes/planets. Now given this consecration of the tiers of the ziggurat it is evident that the notes of the heptachord may have been similarly consecrated. One such reason perhaps, is for the purposes of providing a consecrated heptachord for each day of the week to be used in the music of temple services.

The seven day week has long been thought of as being of Babylonian origin, a result of dividing each lunar month into four weekly periods reflecting the phases of the moon, for the purposes of religious celebrations. Each day of a given seven day week was consecrated to a particular divinity/planet.

However, the order of planets in which they appear in the days of the week is curious, because it does not correspond with their order of ascent in terms of the seven tiers of the ziggurat.

Fig. 5.9: *Connection between Heptachords and Planetary Days of the Week*

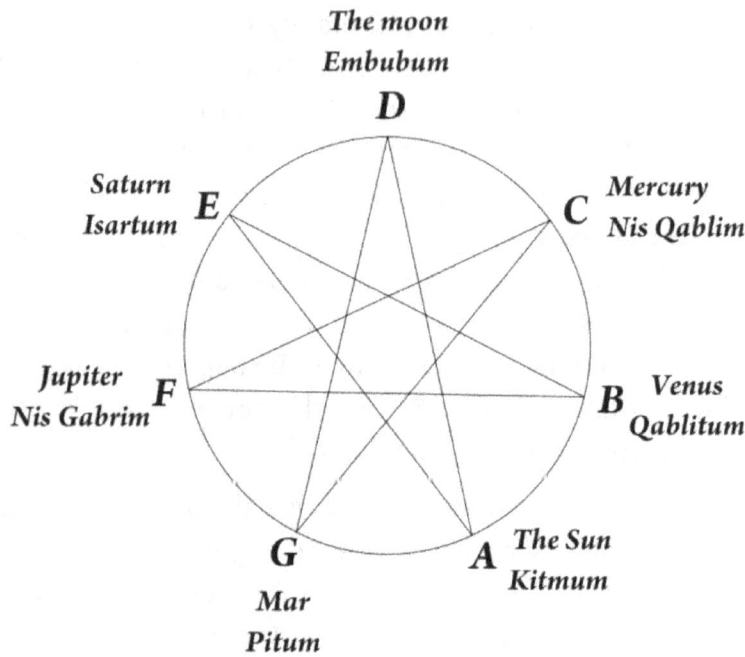

However, Leon Crickmore pointed out that it does exactly correspond with the order of the seven heptachords as they appear in the tuning up/tuning down sequence just discussed.[34] This can be further appreciated by placing the seven notes of the heptachord in their scale-wise order as they occur within the octave circle. The inner heptagon shows their order as they occur, both in terms of the days of the week and the tuning up/down principle (fig. 5.9). Connected with this may be a

---

[34] Leon Crickmore (2013), *Planetary Heptachords and the Days of the Week – the Harmony of the Spheres.*

seven-pointed star engraved within two concentric circles, around whose points are the string names and the numbers 1 through to 7 found on one of the clay tablets.[35] Naturally the interest in this area lies in the possible connection between Babylonian and ancient Greek musical-cosmological models.

[35] Ibid.

6 The Tonoi of Ptolemy

Having considered certain features pertaining to the seven diatonic modes, it now becomes expedient to consider some of the consequences that arose with respect to their possible use in ancient Greek music. The first feature to consider is the obvious connection between mode and modulation.

Mode and modulation...

Although the Greater Perfect System encompassed all seven modes, some of the main instruments of Greek music had a limited range, no more than say an octave. Now given an instrument whose octave range is say note E to E, playing a melody in the Dorian mode would present no problems. However, playing a melody in the Lydian mode would, because the notes in this case range from C to C.

Now as the Greeks had no conception of sharps and flats, in order to be able to play a given mode within the range of the octave from note E to E, the entire Greater Perfect System had to be conceptually shifted up or down in pitch as the case may be, until the selection of notes required for the chosen mode was brought into the playable range of the instrument. Because of this, it became easier to think of the modes as limited sections of a Greater Perfect System built upon a different foundation tone.

These variously necessary pitch shifts of the Greater Perfect System were called *tonoi*, one such shift being called a *tonos*. Although these are sometimes thought of as being keys in a modern sense, conceiving them as keys has unnecessary connotations of tonal centers that are not necessarily implied. They are consequently better thought of as the *tones* upon which a Greater Perfect System might be built.[36] In this context therefore, the words Lydian 'tone' would be the note upon which it would be necessary to build the Greater Perfect System in order to bring the notes of the Lydian mode into the range of the original octave.

Fig. 6.1: *Creation of Lydian Tonos*

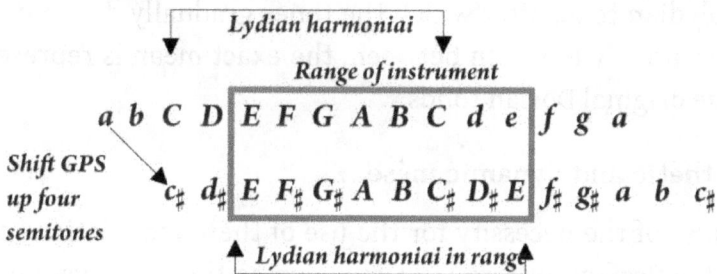

Fig. 6.1 shows this process being applied. The top row of notes represents the Greater Perfect System, while the box represents the single octave range of a lyre. The row of notes at the bottom represents the Greater Perfect System transposed up four semitones – from A up to C sharp. Observe that the Lydian mode

---

[36] Alain Daniélou first suggested this in his *Introduction to the Study of Musical Scales* (1979), p.119.

is now within the playable range of the instrument.

The seven tonoi...

Now although the Greater Perfect System could in theory, be shifted onto any required tone, in his treatise *Harmonics* Claudio Ptolemy argued that there need only be seven tonoi, namely the tones that brought all seven of the modes into a single octave range as defined by the original Dorian mode. Therefore for Ptolemy, the justification for the 'tones' arose primarily from the necessity for transposing the seven modes into the playable range of a given instrument. This can be understood through reference to fig. 6.2 which portrays the seven 'tones', and the way they bring the seven modes into a single octave range, from hypátē meson to nétē diezeugmenon.

In the figure, the bottom note of each key of the Greater Perfect System therefore represents the 'tone'. Note E is therefore the Hypodorian tone, note F sharp the Hypophrygian tone, etc. As can be seen these begin with a relatively high D for the Mixolydian tone, after which the tones gradually descend down to a relatively low E. In between, the exact mean is represented by the original Dorian tonos.

The thetic and dynamic mésē...

Because of the necessity for the use of these modulations of the Greater Perfect System – up or down as the case may be - the central tone, the mésē could be thought of as functioning on two simultaneous levels. First, there was the absolute mésē that Claudio Ptolemy referred to as the *thetic* mésē. Standing at the very heart and centre of the Greater Perfect System, emanating from it were therefore the fixed tones whose ratios derived from the numbers of the Tetractys, the principal numbers that guide and define the natural boundaries of the Greater Perfect System. The absolute or thetic mésē was therefore static, immobile, the fixed centre around which the Greater Perfect System was seen to revolve.

Fig. 6.2: *The Seven Tonoi*

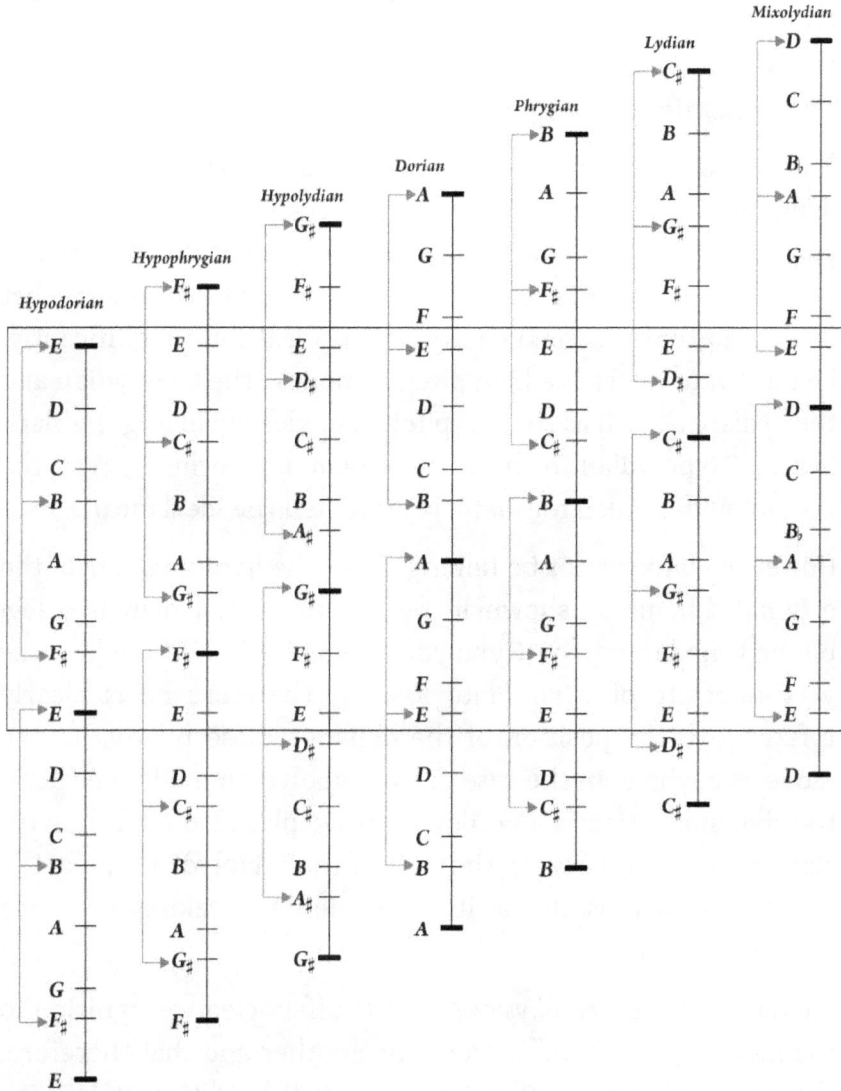

In contrast to the absolute *mésē*, there was the relative or *dynamic* mésē, which rose or fell depending upon the particular harmonia. Bearing in mind that the 'tone' upon which each tonos is built is always an octave down from the dynamic mésē, the scheme of seven tonoi as represented in fig. 6.2, therefore shows a clear picture of a dynamic mésē which extends from a fourth below the thetic mésē in the case of the Hypolydian mode, to a fourth above the thetic mésē in the case of the Mixlydian mode.

The dynamic mésē as contributor to modal ethos...

The sense of tension between a fixed thetic and a mobile dynamic mésē seems to have significantly contributed to the perception of the peculiar ethos or feel that was attributed to particular modes. In the *Republic* Plato discusses the modes that he felt appropriate for the music of his ideal state. Significantly, he tended to reject the high pitched modes- the Mixolydian and the Lydian, as well as the low pitched modes, including the slack Lydian (Hypolydian in the above scheme), favoring instead the Dorian mode, which for Plato, represented the ideal mean.

However Plato cannot be talking about the *harmoniai*, for in the original scheme as shown in fig. 5.1 the Mixolydian is a low pitched mode and the Hypolydian a high pitched mode – the very opposite of what Plato asserts. Therefore he is clearly referring to the position of the dynamic mésē relative to the mode as a whole. In the case of the Hypolydian mode therefore, the dynamic mésē is low down, being placed on a relatively slack string. Similarly, in the case of the Mixolydian mode, the dynamic mésē is as high as it can possibly be, making this mode particularly acute.

Similarly, in his *Metaphysics* Aristotle offers clear recognition to the fact that scales differ from one another and that therefore, the effect of the use of those scales will be different in each case. Indeed, Aristotle even describes some of these effects in which he observes that the Mixolydian mode produces an effect that is sad and grave; the Dorian a moderate and settled temper, while the Phrygian mode inspired enthusiasm. Some modes, he felt, even enfeebled the mind. Omitting to mention what these are, he refers to them simply as relaxed modes, no doubt referring to those modes such as the Hypolydian, whose dynamic mésē is lower in the scale i.e. on a slacker string.[37]

Ptolemy makes similar comments which again, imply a connection between the perceived ethos of a mode and its sense of pitch as reflected by the position of the dynamic mésē. Writing about the effects of melodic modulations, he observes that the higher modes cause an enlivening expression, while the lower modes cause dejection. This he feels, is due to the fact that notes belonging to a high range cause the soul to tense, while notes from a lower range cause the soul to relax. Like Plato, he also refers to the Mixolydian as a high mode and therefore expressing a restless and active sense, and the Hypodorian as a low mode expressing a sense of limpness and dullness.[38]

Characteristics of the seven modes...

Once the seven modes have been transposed into the same octave range they can then be analyzed and compared. The most significant feature is the tetrachord, which for the music of antiquity, carried the status of being a self-contained scale structure in its own right.

From the standpoint of the tetrachordal structure of the seven modes, it is clear that they all derive from a system of diatonic tetrachords, connected either conjunctly or disjunctly. Each

---

[37] Aristotle, *Politics*, 1340a.40.

[38] J. Godwyn, Op. Cit., p. 28.

such tetrachord consists of a perfect fourth that has been divided into two steps of a tone and one of a semitone. Accordingly, there are three possible species of diatonic tetrachord. There is the Dorian tetrachord (fig. 6.3), which in descending order from the mésē proceeds tone, tone, limma:

Fig. 6.3: *Dorian Tetrachord*

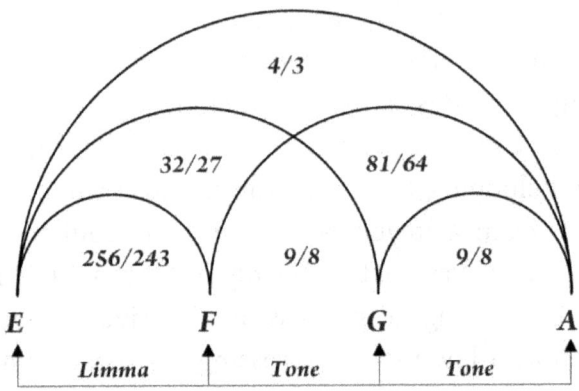

The Phrygian tetrachord, which in descending order from the mésē proceeds tone, limma, tone (Fig. 6.4):

Fig. 6.4: *Phrygian Tetrachord*

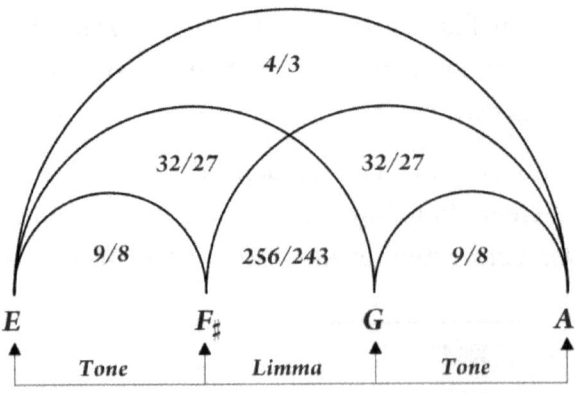

Finally the Lydian tetrachord, which, in descending order from the mésē proceeds limma, tone, tone (Fig. 6.5):

Fig. 6.5: *Lydian Tetrachord*

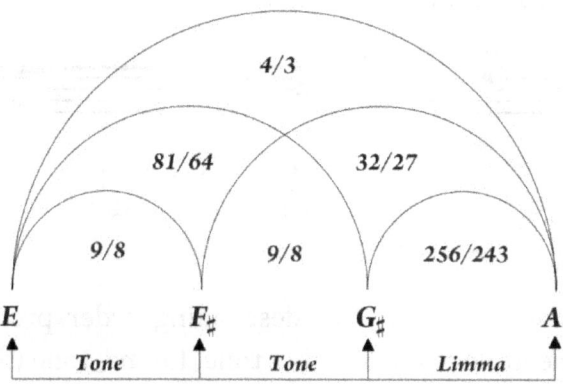

The three main diatonic modes of ancient Greek music are obtained when these three tetrachords are replicated in the tetrachord above.[39] Plutarch referred to this when he wrote of a time when 'the only modes in use were the Dorian, Phrygian and Lydian'.[40] He also claimed that the musician Sarcadas of Argos once composed an ode of three strophes, one in each of the three modes.[41]

This practice of changing mode through the course of a song Plutarch referred to as *mutation*, evidently another term for modulation.[42] Cleonides also speaks of a fourth century lyre that had eleven strings arranged in ten steps that enabled the use of

---

[39] Mathiesen, *Op. Cit*, p. 462.

[40] Plutarch, *On Music*, Sect. 8.

[41] Ibid.

[42] Ibid.

three such harmonia.[43] The three main modes are therefore as follows: the *Dorian mode* consisting of tone, tone, limma, tone of disjunction, tone, tone and limma in descending order (fig. 6.6);

Fig. 6.6: *The Dorian Mode*

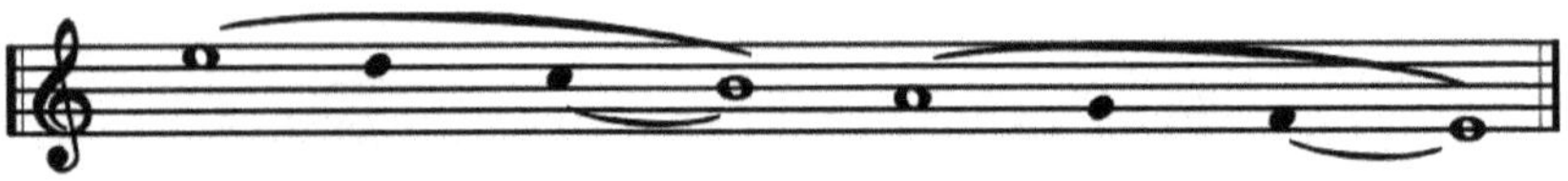

Note:	E	D	C	B	A	G	F	E
Ratio:	2/1	16/9	128/81	3/2	4/3	32/27	256/243	1/1
Cents:	1200	996	792	702	498	294	90	0

the *Phrygian mode* which in descending order proceeds tone, limma, tone, tone of disjunction, tone, limma, tone (fig. 6.7);

Fig. 6.7: *The Phrygian Mode*

Note:	E	D	C♯	B	A	G	F♯	E
Ratio:	2/1	16/9	27/16	3/2	4/3	32/27	9/8	1/1
Cents:	1200	996	906	702	498	294	204	0

the *Lydian mode*, which in descending order proceeds limma, tone, tone, tone of disjunction, limma, tone, tone (fig. 6.8).

Fig. 6.8: *The Lydian Mode*

Note:	E	D♯	C♯	B	A	G♯	F♯	E
Ratio:	2/1	243/128	27/16	3/2	4/3	81/64	9/8	1/1
Cents:	1200	1110	906	702	498	408	204	0

---

[43] Mathiesen, *Op. Cit.*, p. 387.

Observe that all three of these modes use a certain tetrachordal arrangement consisting of an upper and a lower tetrachord separated by a tone of disjunction. This is an important observation because examining the constitution of the Mixolydian mode – the only other mode that does not carry the prefix 'Hypo' – a different tetrachordal arrangement may be immediately discerned. See fig. 6.9.

Fig. 6.9: *The Mixolydian Mode*

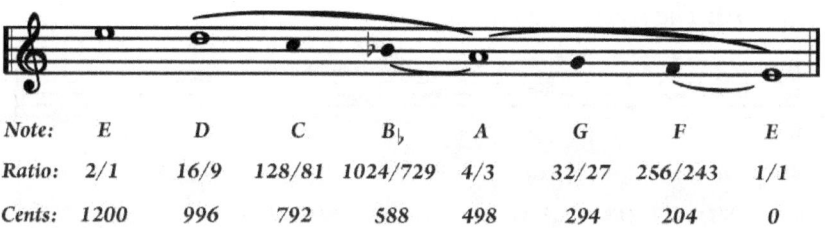

Note:	E	D	C	B♭	A	G	F	E
Ratio:	2/1	16/9	128/81	1024/729	4/3	32/27	256/243	1/1
Cents:	1200	996	792	588	498	294	204	0

The primary indicator is that due to the apparent flattening of paramésē (note B flat) there seems to be no tone of disjunction. As this is impossible within a seven note diatonic scale completed at the octave, it is evident that the Mixolydian mode provides an example of a different species of Dorian tetrachordal arrangement, in which the tetrachords are conjunct, the tone of disjunction now being at the top.

Confirmation of this comes by way of Plutarch who observed that 'Lamprocles of Athens realized that it (the Mixolydian mode) has the disjunctive tone not where almost everyone had been thinking, but at the top and worked out its scheme as being such, as from paramésē down to hypátē hýpaton.'[44] Its characteristic sequence of scale steps therefore proceeds tone, tone, tone, limma, tone, tone, limma.

Another mode, in which the tetrachords seem to take a different form to the three main modes, is the Hypolydian

---

[44] Hagel, *Op. Cit.,* p. 372.

mode. In this case, the mésē is seemingly raised to note A sharp. As the mésē is one of the three fixed tones, this in its turn indicates, that in the case of the Hypolydian mode, yet another tetrachordal arrangement is being implicated in which the tetrachords are also conjunct, except that the original tone of disjunction now lies at the bottom. This results in a mode whose order of scale step sizes is limma, tone, tone, limma, tone, tone, and tone as shown in fig. 6.10.

Fig. 6.10: *The Hypolydian Mode*

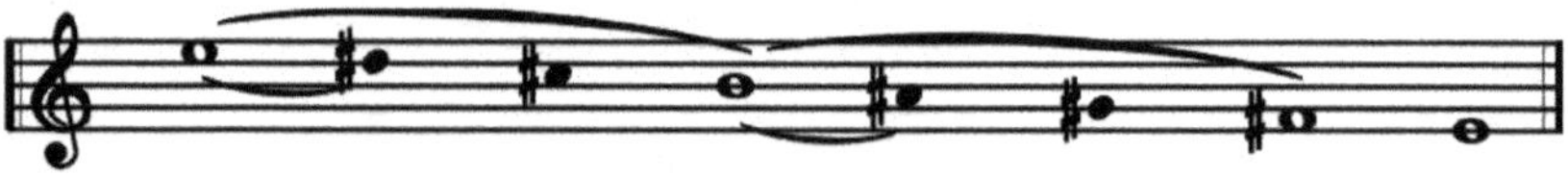

Note:	E	D♯	C♯	B	A♯	G♯	F♯	E
Ratio:	2/1	243/128	27/16	3/2	729/512	81/64	9/8	1/1
Cents:	1200	1110	906	702	612	408	204	0

The other 'Hypo' modes share this tetrachordal structure. These are the Hypodorian mode whose descending order of scale step sizes is tone, tone, semitone, tone, tone, semitone and tone (fig. 6.11).

Fig. 6.11: *The Hypodorian Mode:*

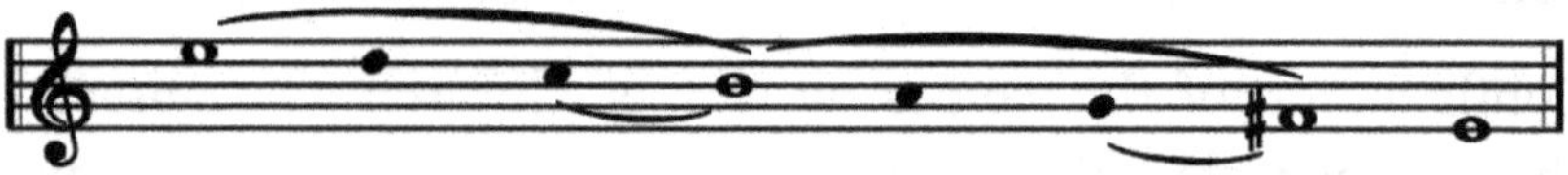

Note:	E	D	C	B	A	G	F♯	E
Ratio:	2/1	16/9	128/81	3/2	4/3	32/27	9/8	1/1
Cents:	1200	996	792	702	498	294	204	0

And the Hypophrygian mode whose order of scale step sizes in descending order is tone, semitone, tone, tone, semitone, tone, and tone (Fig. 6.12).

Fig. 6.12: *The Hypophrygian Mode:*

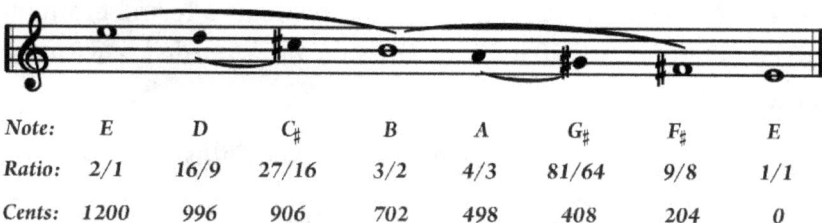

Note:	E	D	C♯	B	A	G♯	F♯	E
Ratio:	2/1	16/9	27/16	3/2	4/3	81/64	9/8	1/1
Cents:	1200	996	906	702	498	408	204	0

As a complete group therefore, all seven modes are composed of a pair of homogenous tetrachords. From the Dorian tetrachord, three such modes are derived: the Dorian, Hypodorian and the Mixolydian; from the Phrygian tetrachord the Phrygian and Hypophrygian modes are derived and from the Lydian tetrachord are derived the Lydian and Hypolydian mode.

The appearance of modes with mixed species of diatonic tetrachords is therefore only apparent, due to the differing placements of the tone of disjunction, either at the bottom of a pair of conjunct tetrachords, between two disjunct tetrachords or above two conjunct tetrachords.

Pythagorean intonation...

Once an awareness has been gained of the main characteristics of the seven modes, it becomes fruitful to consider some of the implications of the use of the modes, particularly in terms of their subsequent impact upon tuning theory. What might be termed the most common method of tuning stringed instruments such as the lyre or cithara, was the Pythagorean method that uses perfect fifths and/or fourths. When this system of tuning is examined in relation to the seven modes it becomes clear that one particular mode could be tuned exclusively in rising fifths/falling fourths:[45] the Hypolydian

---

[45] For the purpose of tuning a rising fifth is equivalent to a falling fourth; similarly a rising fourth is equivalent to a falling fifth.

mode, which derives from a sequence of six fifths up from hypátē. Accordingly each note as it appears as a term belonging to the sequence of fifths may thereby be accorded a ratio, as shown in fig. 6.13a.

Fig. 6.13: *Tuning of Modes using Rising/Falling Fifths*

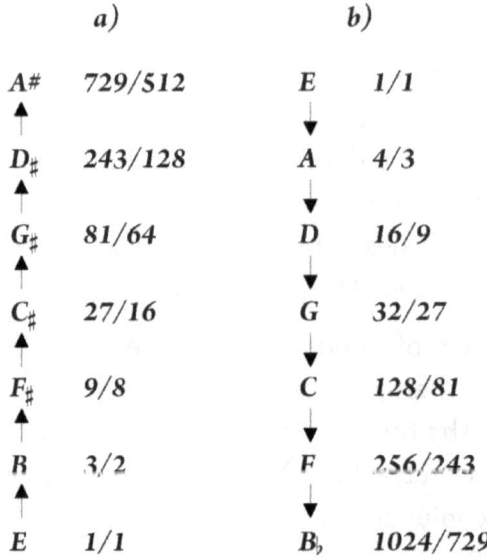

There is also a mode that can be tuned in an opposite sense, that is exclusively according to the lower generation using a sequence of six rising fourths. This is the Mixolydian mode as shown in fig. 6.13b. As the Hypolydian and Mixolydian modes therefore represent two extremes, all seven modes can be derived from a sequence of six rising fifths and fourths as shown in fig. 6. 14.

Examining this scheme causes one to question the logicality of always tuning from the mésē. Clearly tuning from hypátē would be more logical, for while the mésē may have served as the tonal centre, the tuning centre appears to be hypátē, especially since hypátē is thereby the central pivot or fulcrum of the three fixed tones: A, E and B.

Fig. 6.14: *Derivation of Seven Modes from Six Rising Fifths/ Fourths*

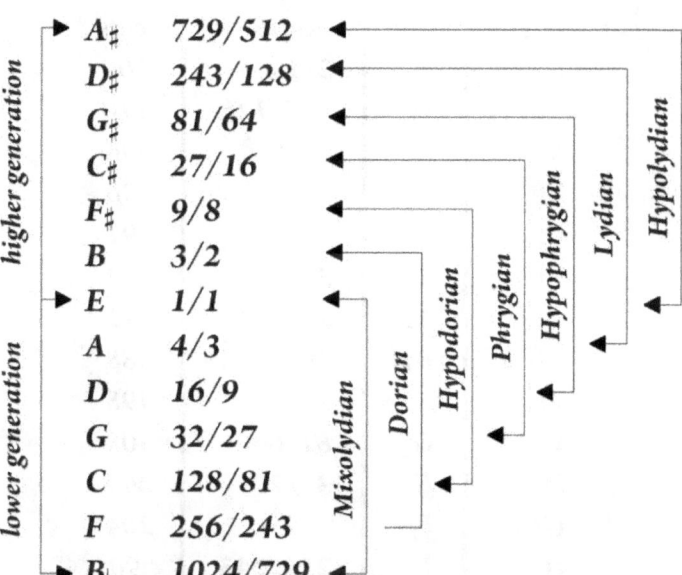

To experiment with the seven modes using the original Pythagorean tuning, the scale needs to be tuned a shown in table 7. A slight problem arises in terms of the double definition of the seventh degree which can appear either as an augmented fourth of ratio 729/512 or a diminished fifth of 1024/729. The former is required for the Hypolydian mode, the latter for the Mixolydian mode. This note would therefore need to be retuned, depending upon which mode was being used.

Table 7: *The Pythagorean Form of Chromatic Scale*

Degree	Note	Ratio	Cents
I	E	2/1	1200
XII	D♯	243/128	1110
XI	D	16/9	996
X	C♯	27/16	906
IX	C	128/81	792
VIII	B	3/2	702
	A♯	729/512	612
VII	B♭	1024/729	588
VI	A	4/3	498
V	G♯	81/64	408
IV	G	32/27	294
III	F♯	9/8	204
II	F	256/243	90
I	E	1/1	0

7 The Shades

As ancient Greek music was conceived as being an essentially melodic art, there was very little interest in either chordal sonorities or the possibilities for chord progressions that underpinned much of Western music. Because of this, the music of antiquity tended to rely instead on a combination of those essentially simple elements that underlie a purely melodic world.

Trying to imagine what that was like, it becomes apparent that exposed for a lifetime to nothing but pure melody, a certain sensitivity to the various fine nuances and shades of melodic expression may develop. This in turn would lead to a difference of theoretical focus, aimed not towards an analysis of the principles of harmony, but towards an understanding of the principles that governed melody and melodic organization, especially in terms of the various ingredients and parameters involved.

The word harmony as used in this context, thus referred not to the use of chords, but to an aesthetic value for order and proportion as crystallized and embodied within the characteristic form of a musical scale. One of the features directly relevant to this was the conception of pitch not in the a priori terms of a musical scale, but as an unbroken continuum of frequencies that stretched from the very heights down to the depths. In between the pitch range thus established, any single point along that continuum may offer a convenient place of rest for the voice. Such resting places – notes - were therefore characterized as points on that continuum.

This is one of the particularly refreshing features of ancient Greek music, because the Western scale today offers only twelve such resting places for the voice within each octave. This arbitrary limitation belies the fact that acoustic nature presents a literally infinite set of choices. Moreover, ancient Greek music was distinguished by the fact that this was not only recognized, but efforts were also made to incorporate some of these flexible possibilities into the musical scales. This in itself undoubtedly gave to ancient Greek melodies a subtle quality of melodic expression that is distinctly absent from most music today.

Chroai...

Another refreshing element was the use of fine-tuning in order to create particular shades of modal colour, which were called *chroai*. To obtain these on the lyre or cithara, Pythagorean tuning would represent only a starting point. Once tuned in this fashion, a fine-tuning process would begin in which certain notes were appreciably 'softened' by a slight relaxation to the tension of the string.

Being used to equal temperament, which offers only a single modal hue, the shades represent a territory which modern Western musicians generally have very little experience. Yet because of this, the exploration of the various shades of modal colour as they applied to the ancient Greek diatonic family of modes, upon modern instruments capable of adapting themselves to fine-tuning, makes for a fascinating subject for further exploration.

Aristoxenus' diatonic modal shades...

A very good place to start this study of the subject of chroai is with the various shades of diatonic modal colour recognized by the philosopher Aristoxenus of Tarentum (fl. 335 B.C.) as explained and discussed in his treatise *Elements of Harmony*. A study of these shades is particularly revealing, not only in terms of the nature of the individual shades themselves, but also for the particular way in which Aristoxenus thought about, envisaged and represented these shades.

The ratios of Pythagoras and his followers are nowhere to be found. Instead, musical notes are conceived as points along a spatial continuum. In this respect, Aristoxenus' approach often comes across as being surprisingly 'modern', finding great accord with modern Western conceptions of musical intervals whose magnitudes can be measured and expressed in terms of cents.

For Aristoxenus, the tone represented a particular focus of interest. Representing the difference between the perfect fifth and the perfect fourth, melodies could employ the resources of the tone, as well as various subdivisions of the tone, among which Aristoxenus makes special mention of half-tones, third-tones and quartertones.

In order to accommodate these subdivisions Aristoxenus thought of the tone as being divisible into twelve parts, of which a semitone would consist of six, a third-tone of four and a quartertone of three. Once the tone had been divided in this manner, he was then able to pinpoint the various positions of the movable notes of the tetrachord to the nearest one-twelfth of a tone. A regular diatonic tetrachord therefore consisted of a tone of twelve parts, another tone of twelve parts and a semitone of six parts, meaning that the perfect fourth would therefore consist of some thirty-parts.

Although by working in this fashion, Aristoxenus was able to dispense with note ratios, in doing so he became particularly vulnerable to criticism, particularly from those who believed that there were major flaws in his arguments. One such flaw was the inferred idea that a semitone is therefore equivalent to half of a whole tone. His critics however, took issue with this inference. The third century neo-Platonic philosopher Porphyry (234 – 305 AD) expressed this criticism in particularly scornful terms, observing that "What is left after taking two whole tones from 4/3 is no more a semitone than a mule is a semi-ass."[46]

Any grounds for this criticism can be easily verified by measuring the whole and half-tone intervals in cents. A diatonic whole tone of ratio 9/8 measures 204 cents, while a diatonic semitone (limma) of ratio 256/243 measures only 90 cents. Two diatonic semitones therefore make 180 cents, some 24 cents short of a whole tone.[47] So it became apparent that Aristoxenus' sums just do not properly add up.

However, this criticism was largely unfair, because Aristoxenus only ever intended to use his system to plot those particular regions where, in actual musical practice, a note was *liable to fall* within the terms of a particular tetrachord. These proximate positions Aristoxenus argued, should be determined not by mathematical ratios, but by the ear. In this sense, his calibrations are not mathematical divisions of the total octave space, but fractions of a functional whole tone whose size was

---

[46] Harry Partch, *Genesis of a Music*, p. 369

[47] This rather small interval is well known to keyboard tuners as the Pythagorean comma of ratio 531441/524288.

itself variable within certain limits.

Indeed, what his critics did not take into account was the fact that the size of the semitone is itself variable. The semitone of 90 cents is only the *minor semitone*; there is also a *major semitone* or apotome of 114 cents. When the average size of these two semitones is considered, a typical semitone therefore works out at 102 cents, exactly half of a whole tone of ratio 9/8 (204 cents)!

Such distractions aside, by dividing the whole tone into twelve theoretical parts, Aristoxenus could represent and compare various shades of modal colour. Among these were two shades of diatonic modal colour: the *intense diatonic* and the *soft diatonic*.

The intense diatonic shade...

Aristoxenus intense diatonic shade divides the perfect fourth into a tone of twelve parts, below which was another tone of twelve parts, at the bottom of which was a semitone of six parts. See fig. 7.1 This shade is clearly meant to be equivalent to the standard diatonic tetrachord obtained by Pythagorean tuning. This type of tuning produced melodic intervals that were discerned aesthetically, as having a rather hard or intense quality, particularly the thirds and the sixths.

Fig. 7.1: *Aristoxenus' Intense Diatonic Tetrachord*

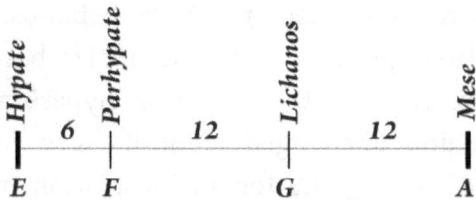

By replicating this tetrachord in the upper half of the octave, the intense diatonic shade of the ancient Greek Dorian mode is obtained, as is illustrated in fig. 7.2. Beneath each of the notes the cents measurements are given:

Fig. 7.2: *Aristoxenus' Intense Diatonic Scale*

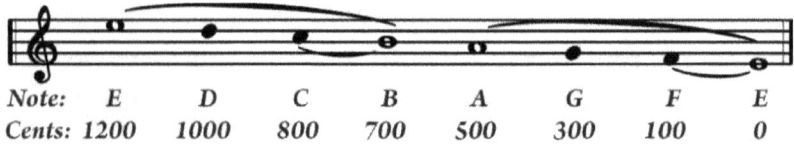

Note:	E	D	C	B	A	G	F	E
Cents:	1200	1000	800	700	500	300	100	0

That Aristoxenus thought of note positions as being variable within certain limits makes the process of assigning cents measurements to his shades somewhat questionable. The cents measurements as shown in fig. 7.2 are therefore only intended as a guide. Even these however, are enough to show that modern Western music is, to all extents and purposes, composed exclusively within the domain of Aristoxenus' intense diatonic shade.

The soft diatonic shade...

As complement to the intense diatonic tetrachord, Aristoxenus also defined a *soft diatonic tetrachord* in which the tetrachord was composed of 15 + 9 + 6 parts (in descending order). In comparison with the intense diatonic tetrachord, the lichanós is flatter by a quarter of a tone, thereby giving the mode a softer, more relaxed feel.

Two consequences of this, are a larger tone of about one and a quarter tones in size between mésē and lichanós, and a smaller tone about three-quarters of a tone in size between lichanós and parhypátē. The semitone between hypátē and parhypátē however, remains unchanged from its size in the intense diatonic shade. See fig. 7.3 for an illustration of Aristoxenus' soft diatonic tetrachord.

Confirmation that scale steps of such sizes were at least recognized in ancient Greek musical practice comes by way of Aristides Quintilianus who observed, "The ancients employed these intervals for the different types of harmoniai. A descent of three incomposite dieses was called eklysis, an ascent of the same interval spondaeiasmos, and an ascent of five dieses, ekbole. These were given names as modification of intervals because of the scarcity of their use".[48]

Fig. 7.3: *Aristoxenus Soft Diatonic Tetrachord*

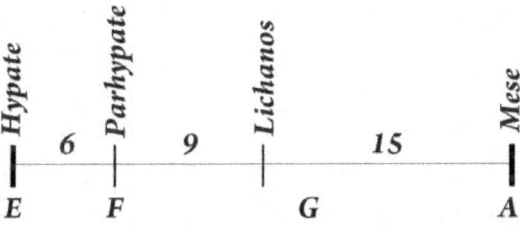

The words 'incomposite dieses' clearly refer to quarter-tones, from which it can be deduced that the three-quarter tone interval that Aristoxenus advocates for the soft diatonic, was once known as an eklysis when falling and a spondaeiasmos on rising; while the five-quartertone interval was known as an ekbole (when falling).

The reason a name was not ascribed to the descending form of the five-quartertone interval is not clear; neither is it clear why different names are ascribed to the same interval, depending upon the direction in which it is taken. Curiously, this distinction did not seem to apply to any other intervals. Possibly this is because ancient Greek modes may have sometimes differed in terms of their rising and falling forms, rather like the modern Western melodic minor mode.

---

[48] Mathiesen, *Op. Cit*, p.538..

Accordingly, a scale step that was a whole tone on descent may have been five-quarters on ascent, etc..

It is interesting to see that scale step sizes of the type referred to by Aristoxenus in the soft diatonic shade are still in use in many parts of the world, especially the three-quarter tone interval, commonly referred to as a neutral tone or neutral second, falling as it does, mid-way in magnitude between the minor second (100 cents) and the major second (200 cents). A neutral tone is illustrated in fig. 7.4. Observe that to notate this scale step, a half-flat sign is needed, which is like a regular flat sign, but with a diagonal stroke drawn through its tail.

Fig. 7.4: *Neutral tone*

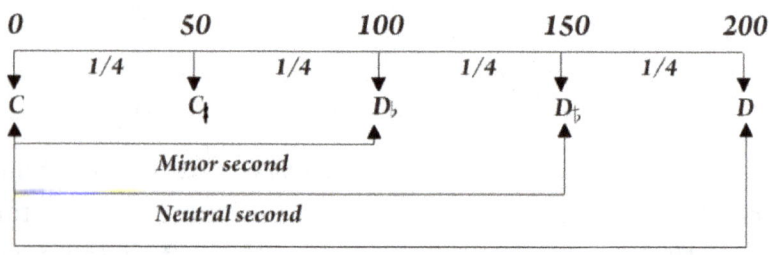

Although unfamiliar to many Western musicians, neutral tones are endemic features of Arabic modal music, where they represent one of the most notable features of the style. They often occur in pairs, dividing a minor third (approx. 300 cents) into two approximately equidistant intervals. Such is the case with the Rast maqam, which bears the same status to Arabic music as did the Dorian mode to Hellenic music.

Use of neutral tones is also typical of the folk music of various European countries, especially those from the East of Europe. However, due to the influence of Western twelve-tone equal temperament, their frequent use has become somewhat obscured, and melodies that commonly used them have simply been re-written to bring them into conformity with Western temperament. Naturally, this represents a great loss for European music.

Using the information Aristoxenus provides about the soft diatonic tetrachord, the soft diatonic form of the ancient Greek Dorian system may be obtained by replicating the soft diatonic tetrachord above the tone of disjunction (fig. 7.5).

Fig. 7.5: *Aristoxenus Soft Diatonic Scale System*

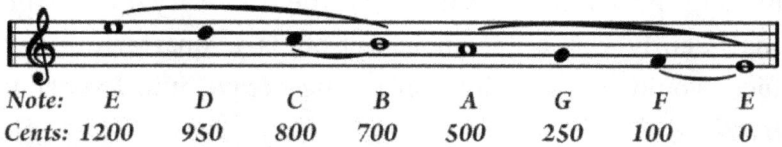

Note:	E	D	C	B	A	G	F	E
Cents:	1200	950	800	700	500	250	100	0

Observe that while Aristoxenus' intense diatonic scale uses only two sizes of scale steps, his soft diatonic uses four, scale steps of 100 cents (semitone); 150 cents (three-quarter-tone); 200 cents (whole tone) and 250 cents (five-quarter-tone). These may be viewed within a circular format, as shown in fig. 7.6.

Fig. 7.6: *Scale Step Sizes in Aristoxenus' Soft Diatonic*

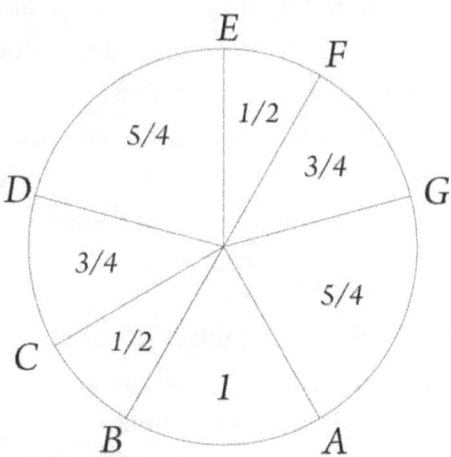

Aristoxenus' soft diatonic shade presents some interesting possibilities in terms of the seven modes that may be derived from it. Indeed, as the soft diatonic is cast up as a shade of the diatonic species, there is no reason to believe that, on a par with the regular intense diatonic shade, that the terms of the soft diatonic shade are not applicable to all of the modes. This prospect however, presents an interesting predicament to modern musicians. What type of foundation scale would be needed in order to be able to play all seven modes within a single octave range? Clearly a chromatic scale would not be sufficient, because it does not yield the necessary quartertones. Consequently the only viable option is a quartertone scale, which would imply a division of the octave into twenty-four parts.

Bearing this in mind, if, during an earlier age in the development of Western music, the shades had not been excluded from general use, our music today might have been very different. For while our study of Aristoxenus' soft diatonic shade may be firmly embedded within the context of the historical study of ancient Greek musical scales, it cannot be denied that outside of that particular context, the quartertone scale that it invokes represents a universal scalar possibility that musicians from all cultures may draw upon should they choose. Arabic modal music provides a useful measure of success with regard to the use of a quartertone scale, for that use both supports and facilitates the free use of a set of melodic modes whose provenance would indeed seem to go all the way back to the times of ancient Greece.

Utilizing the fine tuning capabilities of an electronic keyboard, it may not be possible to play a scale of quarter-tones, but it is possible to tune any of the seven modes belonging to the soft diatonic shade of Aristoxenus, as fig. 7.7 clearly shows. Consulting this figure shows that Aristoxenus soft diatonic scale makes almost full use of the resources of a quartertone scale:

Microtonality in Ancient Greek Music

Fig. 7.7: *Tuning for the Seven Modes Using Aristoxenus' Soft Diatonic Shade*

Degree	Note	Cents	Dorian	Phrygian	Lydian	Mixolydian	Hypodorian	Hypophrygian	Hypolydian
1	E	1200	●	●	●	●	●	●	●
24	E♭	1150							
23	D♯	1100			●				●
22	D!	1050		●				●	
21	D	1000				●			
20	D♭	950	●	●			●	●	
19	C♯	900			●				
18	C!	850							●
17	C	800	●			●			
16	C♭	750		●	●				
15	B	700	●				●	●	●
14	B♭	650				●			
13	A♯	600					●		●
12	A!	550						●	
11	A	500	●	●	●	●			
10	A♭	450					●	●	●
9	G♯	400			●				
8	G!	350	●						
7	G	300					●		
6	G♭	250	●	●		●	●		
5	F♯	200					●		
4	F!	150		●					●
3	F	100	●			●			
2	F♭	50							
1	E	0	●	●	●	●	●	●	●

When examining this scale, and the modal possibilities that it embraces, an immediate problem of nomenclature arises. Western music theory generally stops short at the chromatic scale of semitones. Consequently, there is no generally accepted nomenclature used to describe and represent the various intervals encountered in quartertone or indeed, other types of microtonal scale.

With certain degrees of the scale the use of the term neutral is clearly applicable, the meaning and sense of this term being an interval that is somewhere between major and minor. This applies to the fourth degree where a neutral second appears; the eighth degree which clearly represents a neutral third; the eighteenth degree which is a neutral sixth and the twenty-second degree which is a neutral seventh.

8 Diatonic Shades of Ptolemy

Because Aristoxenus' shades are expressed through the theoretical terms of his own system, it is sometimes difficult to discern the harmonic logic behind them. To gain a clearer idea of this logic, it therefore becomes useful to cross-reference what Aristoxenus has to say on the shades, with information provided by other philosophers and theorists who were less shy of note ratios.

Probably the most important source of information on this subject is Claudius Ptolemy, (90 A.D. – 168 A.D.), an Alexandrian philosopher who wrote on a wide range of subjects including geography, astrology, astronomy, mathematics and an important work on the music of antiquity, *Harmonics*.

Being aware of an acute sense of conflict between the proponents of Aristoxenus on the one hand and Pythagoras on the other, his work argues for a balance that both recognizes the need for empirical investigation, yet at the same time is also capable of embracing the mathematics of the Pythagoreans.

A value for epimoric ratios...

One of the salient features underlying Ptolemy's approach to the shades and the process of tuning in general, is a marked preference for the use of super-particular ratios (epimores). An epimore may be defined as a ratio in which the numerator exceeds the denominator by unity. The ratios of the primary intervals of the octave (2/1), perfect fifth (3/2), perfect fourth (4/3) and whole tone (9/8) are therefore all examples of epimores.

Although epimoric ratios clearly had a significance in terms of Pythagorean number lore, as construed in a more modern sense, they represent striking examples of musical intervals that conform to adjacent terms of the harmonic series 1:2:3:4:5:6:7:8:9: etc.. As such, scale steps bound by epimoric ratios are not only endorsed by the natural configuration of the musical tone, but they are also in accord with the way in which musical instruments naturally tend to vibrate. Therefore, it could easily be argued that scale divisions based on epimores are entirely in conformity with the harmonic logic of the musical tone.

Ptolemy also shows no hesitation in going beyond the numerical limits of the Tetractys in order to achieve a satisfactory tuning for a particular scale. Indeed, for these purposes Ptolemy employs intervals whose ratios extend well beyond the prime number three limit imposed by the Tetractys, advocating as he does, advantageous use of the prime numbers five, seven and eleven as well.

Ptolemy's ditonal diatonic shade..

Like Aristoxenus before him, Ptolemy defined a basic shade of the diatonic scale based on the principles of Pythagorean tuning, which he called the *ditonal diatonic* shade. The tetrachord therefore consisted of two whole tones of ratio 9/8 and a limma of ratio 256/243 in descending order.

Viewing the scale as thus tuned, it becomes apparent that although the relationships between adjacent degrees of the scale possess a consistent mathematical logic, as an organic sum of relationships centered around a modal tonic, Pythagorean tuning does not necessarily produce the most desirable outcome. This is for a number of reasons.

Viewing the individual notes of the ditonal diatonic shade in terms of their relationship to the modal tonic, it becomes apparent that in many cases, the notes of the scale express only a very distant relationship to it. Therefore the minor thirds have a relatively complex ratio of 32/27, the minor sixths 128/81, the major thirds 81/64 and the major sixths 27/16. These are not necessarily the most harmonious forms of these intervals that were known to ancient Greek musicians. As such, their use is not necessarily the best choice in all possible contexts.

Furthermore, if the relationships that bind together various segments of the scale consisting of adjacent scale steps are examined, it becomes apparent that these relationships are also rather distant ones. Therefore, two adjacent scale steps are bound either by a trihemitone of 32/27, or by a Pythagorean ditone of ratio 81/64 – rather complex relationships, while three whole tone steps are bound by the even more complex Pythagorean tritone of 729/512. Hence the characteristic 'hardness' of Pythagorean tuning, which is entirely due to the opacity of the internal relationships between the notes of the scale. This opacity is a direct symptom of the relative complexity of the ratios used.

Ptolemy's intense diatonic shade...

Although conforming to the general profile of the diatonic scale as produced by Pythagorean tuning, Ptolemy's intense diatonic shade represents the application of mathematical logic to try to solve some of the problems that have already been outlined. Therefore the relationships of the various notes of the scale to the modal tonic tend to use much simpler ratios, thereby offering a more close-knit harmony, as indeed do the major and minor thirds that serve to bind various pairs of adjacent scale steps into a more harmonious relationship with one another.

In order to accomplish this Ptolemy gives himself leeway to use intervals whose ratios use prime numbers higher than three. Although this automatically places his solutions outside of the limiting framework of the Tetractys, it nonetheless enabled Ptolemy to use intervals with much simpler ratios, thereby enabling his shades to create a much closer knit harmony.

One of the central cruxes of the problem for Ptolemy was dividing the perfect fourth, whose extremities bounded the tetrachord, into a series of intervals whose ratios were all epimores. In order to accomplish this Ptolemy replaced the Pythagorean ditone (81/64 - 408 c.) between mésē and parhypátē with the 'sweeter' sounding major third of ratio 5/4.

This move was no doubt suggested by the knowledge that deducting unity from the denominator of the ratio of the ditone (81/64), resulted in a much simpler ratio of 80/64 (80/64 = 5/4 - 386 c.). Applying this to the interval between mésē and parhypátē, this left the much more desirable epimoric minor second (16/15 - 112 c.) between parhypátē and hypátē.

The next step was to multiply 5/4 by two to produce 10/8. By selecting the arithmetic mean between eight and ten, the epimoric major third was thereby divided into a major tone (9/8

– 204 c.) and a minor tone (10/9 – 182 c.). Parhypátē, lichanós and mésē were thereby bound into a more mathematically logical 8/9/10 relationship - conforming to the eighth, ninth and tenth harmonics. Ptolemy's logic in this respect can be appreciated through reference to the illustration of his intense diatonic tetrachord provided for in fig. 8.1:

Fig. 8.1: *Ptolemy's Intense Diatonic Tetrachord*

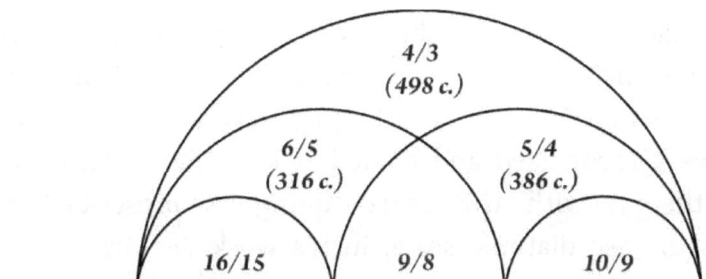

As thus tuned, Ptolemy's intense diatonic shade yields a Dorian scale system in which only one ratio requires any number beyond the numbers of the decade. The limma of ratio 256/243 has been replaced by the diatonic semitone of ratio 16/15; the Pythagorean minor third of ratio 32/27 by the harmonic minor third of ratio 6/5; the Pythagorean minor sixth of ratio 128/81 has been replaced by the harmonic minor sixth of ratio 8/5 and the Pythagorean minor seventh of ratio 16/9 by the harmonic minor seventh of ratio 9/5. In each case, an interval with a complex ratio has been replaced by one with a simpler ratio. Yet the overall profile of the scale also remains basically unchanged. See fig. 8.2 for an illustration of this scale.

Fig. 8.2: *Ptolemy's Intense Diatonic Dorian System*

Note:	E	D	C	B	A	G	F	E
Ratio:	2/1	9/5	8/5	3/2	4/3	6/5	16/15	1/1
Cents:	1200	1018	814	702	498	316	112	0

The ingenuity of Ptolemy's formulation for the intense diatonic system is readily apparent in the way that it anticipates the just intonation principles of later European theorists. Therefore Johann Kirnberger (1721 – 1783), lists the seven diatonic modes as they were recognized and named at the time in European musical theory, with the exact tuning as prescribed by Ptolemy's intense diatonic scale, in his work *The Art of Strict Musical Composition.*[49]

However, for a modern realization of the seven diatonic modes using Ptolemy's intense diatonic tuning, a chromatic scale of twelve-tones to the octave is not enough. Ptolemy's tuning requires a subtle distinction to be made between enharmonically distinct forms of the same interval. A good example of this, is that in the Phrygian mode the second degree has a ratio of 10/9, which is the minor tone of 182 cents, while in the Lydian mode the second degree has a ratio of 9/8 – the major tone of 204 cents. The difference between these two is a tiny snippet of a tone known to tuners as the comma of Didymus (81/80 – 22 cents).

---

[49] Kirnberger's tuning itself however, is clearly derived from the earlier sixteenth century Italian theorist Gioseffo Zarlino's original tuning for the Ionian mode.

Fig. 8.3: *The Seven Modes Tuned Using Ptolemy's Intense Diatonic Shade*

	Note	Ratio	Cents	Dorian	Phrygian	Lydian	Mixolydian	Hypodorian	Hypophrygian	Hypolydian
1	E	2/1	1200	●	●	●	●	●	●	●
19	D♯	15/8	1188			●				●
18	D	9/5	1018	●				●		
17	D	16/9	996		●		●		●	
16	C♯	27/16	906			●				●
15	C♯	5/3	884	●				●		
14	C	8/5	814	●			●	●		
13	B	3/2	702	●		●		●	●	●
12	B	40/27	680		●					
11	B♭	64/45	610				●			
10	A♯	45/32	590							●
9	A	27/20	520					●		
8	A	4/3	498	●	●	●	●		●	
7	G♯	5/4	386			●			●	●
6	G	6/5	316	●			●	●		
5	G	32/27	294		●					
4	F♯	9/8	204			●	●			●
3	F♯	10/9	182		●				●	
2	F	16/15	112	●			●			
1	E	1/1	0	●	●	●	●	●	●	●

Therefore an *enharmonic scale* is required, that is to say a scale which, in this particular instance, uses some nineteen tones to the octave. This scale, together with the tuning needed for each of the seven modes is shown in fig. 8.3. In modern equal temperament, all such intervals that are enharmonically distinct are considered to be rounded off to the nearest one hundred cents interval. Hence their specific modal identities are reduced to a common enharmonically equivalent identity that is meant by proxy, to represent them all.

Although this greatly simplifies the scale system, it nonetheless fails to account for the enharmonic distinctions between intervals which are often the most potent and expressive features of modal systems of music. This will soon become apparent when efforts are made to apply fine-tuning in order to be able to play and experiment with these modes as tuned in accordance with Ptolemy's intense diatonic shade.

Didymus' diatonic tuning...

Ptolemy's tuning solution to the intense diatonic tetrachord is very similar to that which he lists under and accredits to Didymus (see fig. 8.4). The only difference is that the latter places the minor tone (10/9) as the central step of the tetrachord, while Ptolemy placed it uppermost. For Didymus therefore, this led to the retention of the Pythagorean minor third of ratio 32/27 and the Pythagorean minor sixth of ratio 16/9. Otherwise, both Ptolemy's and Didymus' versions of the intense diatonic are very similar.

Fig. 8.4: *Didymus' Diatonic Tuning*

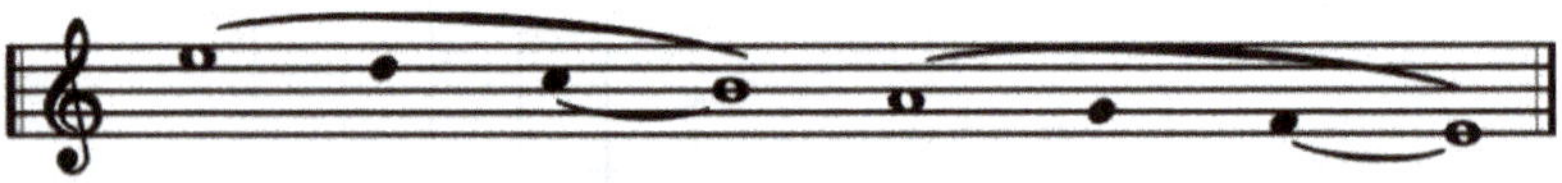

Note:	E	D	C	B	A	G	F	E
Ratio:	2/1	16/9	8/5	3/2	4/3	32/27	16/15	1/1
Cents:	1200	996	814	702	498	294	112	0

Ptolemy's soft diatonic shade..

Ptolemy also offers a prescription for the soft diatonic shade, a shade whose general profile has already been considered in Aristoxenian terms in the last chapter. Aristoxenus' soft diatonic shade involved a slight lowering of lichanós, to the extent of producing a neutral tone (3/4 of a tone) between lichanós and hypátē, thereby enlarging the upper tone of the tetrachord by as much as a quarter of a tone.

No doubt being aware of Aristoxenus' profile for the soft diatonic tetrachord, Ptolemy applies his mathematical skills in order to create the most musically logical solution to the problem posed i.e. how to produce a soft diatonic tetrachord using epimoric ratios. This tetrachord is illustrated in fig. 8.5.

Fig. 8.5: *Ptolemy's Soft Diatonic Tetrachord*

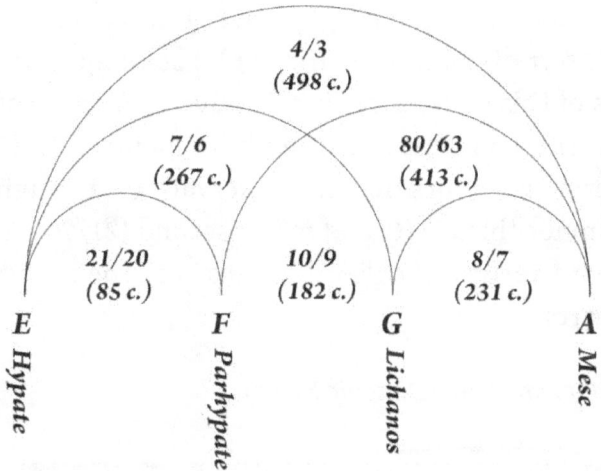

Notice the use of the prime number seven, the primary generator of what are today termed septimal intervals. In terms of the harmonic series, septimal intervals begin with the appearance of the seventh harmonic, which places itself between the sixth and eighth harmonics, thereby dividing the perfect fourth into two intervals whose ratios are 7/6 and 8/7.

Observe that Ptolemy advantageously uses these in his division of the perfect fourth, invoking as he does, the large septimal tone that appropriately lowers the pitch of the lichanós in such a way as to produce the characteristic profile of the soft diatonic tetrachord. In order to divide the remaining septimal interval 7:6 (between lichanós and hypátē) he then multiplies the ratio by 3 to produce 21:18 and then inserts 20 as a mean between the two terms.

The result is a logical division of the septimal interval 7/6 into a minor tone of 10/9 and a small septimal semitone of 21/20. The only defect so far as Ptolemy must have been concerned, is the relatively unwieldy septimal form of major third whose ratio is 80/63 (between mésē and parhypátē), an interval only 5 cents larger than the Pythagorean ditone.

When extended over the range of both tetrachords the result is Ptolemy's soft diatonic scale (fig. 8.6). Looking at the ratios for the notes of this scale, there is a relative abundance of septimal intervals. These include the seventh harmonic itself (7/4) along with septimal colours for the intervals of the minor sixth (63/40), minor third (7/6) and minor second (21/20). All of these offer characteristically 'soft' forms of their Pythagorean counterparts.

Fig. 8.6: *Ptolemy's Soft Diatonic System*

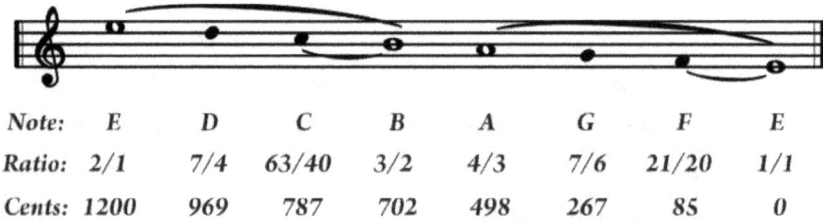

Note:	E	D	C	B	A	G	F	E
Ratio:	2/1	7/4	63/40	3/2	4/3	7/6	21/20	1/1
Cents:	1200	969	787	702	498	267	85	0

Fig. 8.7 shows the scale step sizes used in this scale. These include some three varieties of whole tone, which are the minor tone of ratio 10/9 – 182 cents); the major tone of ratio 9/8 (204 cents) and what is sometimes called the maximum tone of ratio 8/7 (231 cents). This means that the total number of notes needed for the full realization of all seven modes within this

particular shade is twenty-six as fig. 8.8 shows.

Fig. 8.7 *Scale Step Sizes in Ptolemy's Soft Diatonic System*

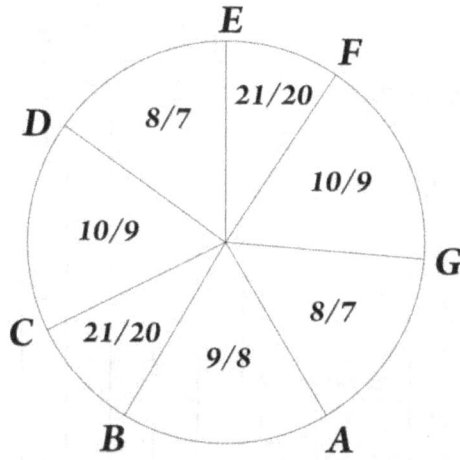

Ptolemy's whole-tone diatonic shade...

A third diatonic shade recognized by Ptolemy was the *whole-tone diatonic* shade, whose characteristic feature was an appreciable softening of parhypátē so that its pitch falls much closer to the bottom note of the tetrachord hypátē. One of the consequences of this is the enlargement of the tone between lichanós and parhypátē. To accomplish this Ptolemy uses the large septimal major third (9/7) between mésē and parhypátē.

Being slightly larger than the regular Pythagorean ditone, it thereby leads to that necessary softening of parhypátē. Ptolemy divides this interval (9/7) using the arithmetic mean eight, which results in the regular Pythagorean whole tone (9/8) at top and the large septimal tone beneath it. This leaves the small septimal semitone 28/27 at the bottom of the tetrachord. The result is that the entire tetrachord can then be represented by the number series 27:28:32:36.

Fig. 8.8: *Tuning for the Seven Modes in Ptolemy's Soft Diatonic Shade*

Note		Ratio	Cents	Dorian	Phrygian	Lydian	Mixolydian	Hypodorian	Hypophrygian	Hypolydian
1	E	2/1	1200	●	●	●	●	●	●	●
26	D♯	40/21	1115		●					●
25	D	9/5	1018		●		●	●		
24	D	16/9	996							
23	D	7/4	969	●				●		
23	C♯	12/7	932		●			●		
22	C♯	320/189	911			●				
21	C♯	5/3	884							●
20	C	63/40	787	●			●			
19	C	14/9	765					●		
18	B	32/21	729		●					
17	B	3/2	702	●				●	●	●
16	B	40/27	680			●				
15	A♯	10/7	617							●
14	A♯	7/5	583				●			
13	A	27/20	520						●	
12	A	4/3	498	●	●	●				
11	A	21/16	471					●		
10	G♯	9/7	435						●	
9	G♯	80/63	413			●				●
8	G	6/5	316		●					
7	G	189/160	289					●		
6	G	7/6	267	●			●			
5	F♯	8/7	231		●				●	
4	F♯	9/8	204					●		
3	F♯	10/9	182			●				●
2	F	21/20	85	●			●			
1	E	1/1	0	●	●	●	●	●	●	●

In his formulation for this tetrachord, Ptolemy's solution agrees with a much earlier formulation for the diatonic tetrachord as originally recommended by Archytas. See fig. 8.9 for an illustration of this.

Fig. 8.9: *Ptolemy's Whole Tone Diatonic Tetrachord*

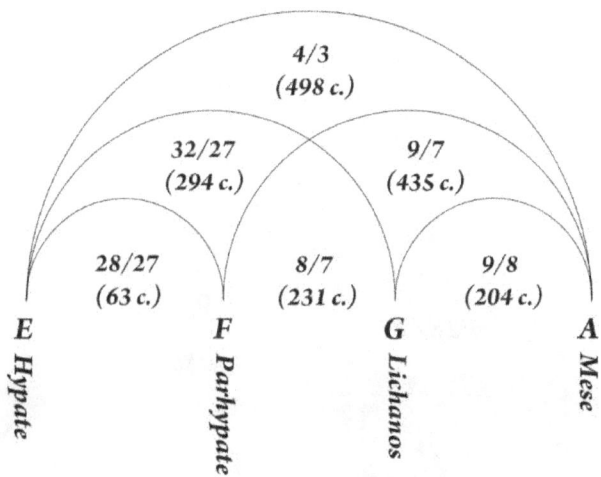

The result is a tetrachord in which all three scale steps are bound by epimoric ratios. The complete Dorian scale system obtained by adding in the implied upper tetrachord appears as shown in fig. 8.10.

Fig. 8.10: *Ptolemy's Whole Tone Scale System*

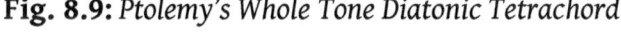

Note:	E	D	C	B	A	G	F	E
Ratio:	2/1	16/9	14/9	3/2	4/3	32/27	28/27	1/1
Cents:	1200	996	765	702	498	294	63	0

This scale uses three scale step sizes – the septimal diesis of 28/27 between the first and second; fifth and sixth degrees; the large septimal whole tone between the second and third; sixth and seventh degrees, the remaining scale steps being taken up by regular whole tones of ratio 9/8. These are illustrated in fig. 8.11.

Fig. 8.11: *Scale Step Sizes in Ptolemy's Whole Tone Diatonic System*

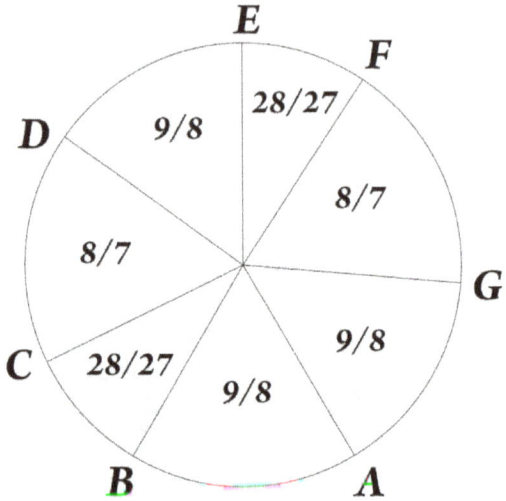

This system represents a fascinating study of septimal methods of tuning. The harmonic major and minor thirds and sixths which Ptolemy used in his intense diatonic shade are nowhere to be found. The minor thirds are either Pythagorean (32/27) or septimal (7/6); the major thirds are also either Pythagorean (81/64) or septimal (9/7). The same applies to their inversions in terms of the minor and major sixths.

To embrace the tuning for all seven modes using Ptolemy's whole tone diatonic shade a scale system is implied uses some twenty-one notes to the octave, a scale illustrated in fig. 8.12.

Microtonality in Ancient Greek Music

Fig. 8.12: *Tuning of the Seven Modes in Ptolemy's Whole Tone Diatonic System*

Note		Ratio	Cents	Dorian	Phrygian	Lydian	Mixolydian	Hypodorian	Hypophrygian	Hypolydian
1	E	2/1	1200	●	●	●	●	●	●	●
21	D♯	27/14	1137			●				●
20	D	16/9	996	●			●	●		
19	D	7/4	969		●				●	
18	C♯	12/7	933			●				●
17	C♯	27/16	906	●					●	
16	C	128/81	792				●			
15	C	14/9	765	●				●		
14	B	32/21	729		●					
13	B	3/2	702	●	●			●	●	●
12	A♯	81/56	639							●
11	B♭	112/81	561				●			
10	A	4/3	498	●	●	●	●			
9	A	21/16	471						●	
8	G♯	9/7	435			●				●
7	G♯	81/64	408						●	
6	G	32/27	294	●				●		
5	G	7/6	267		●			●		
4	F♯	8/7	231			●				●
3	F♯	9/8	204	●				●	●	
2	F	28/27	63	●				●		
1	E	1/1	0	●	●	●	●	●	●	●

Ptolemy's equable diatonic...

Among the various diatonic shades recognized by Ptolemy, his equable diatonic counts as one of the most interesting, yet curious tunings presented by him. In order to obtain the equable tetrachord Ptolemy simply multiplies the ratio of the perfect fourth by 3 to produce 12:9, taking all of the intervening numbers to be the positions of the notes of the tetrachord. This enables Ptolemy to realize a tuning for the tetrachord in which the three intervals are very similar in breadth, although as the scale descends a graceful natural curve of diminishing scale-step sizes occurs. Indeed, when the whole tone spanning the paramésē - mésē disjunction is taken into account (9/8), this produces a notable progression of super-particular ratios – 9/8 – 10/9 – 11/10 – 12/11. See fig. 8.13.

Fig. 8.13: *Ptolemy's Equable Diatonic Tetrachord*

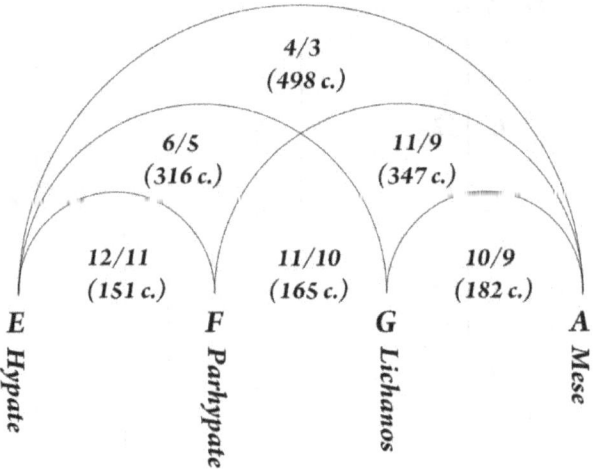

Extended over the range of two tetrachords this produces the scale as shown in fig. 8.14. Expressible by the series of whole numbers 18:20:22:24:27:30:33:36, this scale is commendable for its arithmetic. However, does it represent a real tuning or simply a mathematical exercise?

Fig. 8.14: *Ptolemy's Equable Diatonic Scale*

Note:	E	D	C	B	A	G	F	E
Ratio:	2/1	9/5	18/11	3/2	4/3	6/5	12/11	1/1
Cents:	1200	1018	853	702	498	316	151	0

In answer to this question Ptolemy himself described this tuning as having a 'rather foreign and boorish character, but otherwise it is gentle, and especially when practiced by the ear'.[50] Using a tetrachord that approximates to a tone followed by two three-quarter tones, this tuning does resemble one of the standard ways in which the Greek aulos was bored at one time.[51] Helmholtz however, saw in it a trumpet scale, using as it does, adjacent intervals of the harmonic series.[52] However, as these would belong to a sub-harmonic series, it is difficult to see how Helmholtz arrives at this conclusion. Ptolemy's equable diatonic has also been used effectively in Arabic music, where it is known as the Husayni makam. A similar type of tuning is also used in some of the folk music of Georgia, although this tuning is arrived at by dividing the fourths that bound the two tetrachords into three approximately equal intervals. Although these are all isolated examples, they do show that the equable diatonic is not a scale that Ptolemy simply pulled out of his hat.

To obtain all seven modes within the same octave range an extended scale would be required which in this case, has twenty-six notes. Due to the small differences of tonal range, as

---

[50] Mathiesen, Op. Cit. p.

[51] Hagel, Op. Cit., p. 156.

[52] Helmholtz, *On The Sensations of Tone*, p. 454.

seen for example between in the minute difference of magnitudes between the scale steps of ratio 12/11, 11/10 and 10/9, this scale is therefore characterized by a series of large gaps on the one hand, and compressed regions of adjacent microtones on the other. See fig. 8.15 for a representation of this scale.

Using over a dozen intervals whose ratios involve the prime number eleven, clearly this particular prime number plays a powerful role in determining the general character and feel of the equable diatonic scale. Indeed, each of Ptolemy's shades tends to derive its main characteristics from the prime numbers invoked by the ratios of the intervals used. In the case of his ditonal diatonic shade the salient prime number is three, that is Pythagorean tuning. In his intense diatonic shade the salient prime number five. In both his soft diatonic and whole diatonic shade the salient prime number is seven while in his equable diatonic shade the salient prime number is eleven. In this way Ptolemy makes effective use of those prime numbers which, being the closest to unity, generate the most powerful and resonant intervallic relationships.

Microtonality in Ancient Greek Music

Fig. 8.15: *Tuning of the Seven Modes in Ptolemy's Equable Diatonic Shade*

	Note	Ratio	Cents	Dorian	Phrygian	Lydian	Mixolydian	Hypodorian	Hypophrygian	Hypolydian
1	E	2/1	1200	●	●	●	●	●	●	●
27	D♯	11/6	1049			●				●
26	D	20/11	1034	●					●	
25	D	9/5	1018	●			●			
24	D	16/9	996			●				
23	C♯	5/3	884		●			●		
22	C♯	33/20	867							●
21	C	18/11	853	●				●		
20	C	44/27	845			●				
19	C	8/5	814				●			
18	B	3/2	702	●				●	●	●
17	B	40/27	680		●					
16	B	22/15	663			●				
15	B	16/11	649				●			
14	A	11/8	551							●
13	A	30/22	537						●	
12	A	27/20	520					●		
11	A	4/3	498	●	●	●	●			
10	G♯	5/4	386						●	
9	G	27/22	355					●		
8	G	11/9	347			●				●
7	G	40/33	333		●					
6	G	6/5	316	●				●		
5	F♯	9/8	204					●		
4	F♯	10/9	182		●				●	
3	F	11/10	165			●				●
2	F	12/11	151	●			●			
1	E	1/1	0	●	●	●	●	●	●	●

9 The Chromatic Genus

The different modal colours examined so far offer a fascinating insight into the wealth and complexity of the ancient Greek scale system. One of the great strengths of that system is that the movable notes of the tetrachord could be positioned quite flexibly, thereby giving rise to distinct modal shades that in Western music at least, have mostly been long forgotten.

Here it is interesting to make a comparison between ancient Greek music and modern Western music, for it becomes apparent that, compared to the music of ancient Greece, modern Western music is poverty stricken by way of the possible shades of scales that might advantageously be used.

Indeed, once the shades are known, then it is clear to see that the modes of Western music are all essentially monochromatic, a shade that in its tempered version at least, glints like cold hard steel. Experimenting with the different shades of ancient Greek modes therefore, offers a refreshing alternative to playing and composing music using just one modal shade.

Indeed, once the shades are known about, it becomes apparent that through its adherence to equal temperament, the music of the West is imposing an unnecessary restriction upon itself. Who knows what beautiful melodies might yet be composed using these ancient modes and scales?

However, so far only the *diatonic* family of modes have been considered. There are a further two families of ancient Greek modes yet to be considered, these being the *chromatic* and the *enharmonic*. Together with the diatonic genus, these fall under the collective heading of *genera*. Some of the most fascinating features of Greek modal theory arise with respect to the genera, although like much else with ancient Greek music, many of these features, particularly those surrounding the use of these scales. are rather enigmatic and elusive. However, knowledge that is available so far, at least offers an opportunity for reconstructing these scales, and thereby also the opportunity for even making use of them. In the next couple of chapters therefore, the constitution of both the chromatic and enharmonic genus will be examined, together with their respective shades and colours, beginning with the chromatic genus first.

The constitution of the chromatic tetrachord...

The crux of the three genera lies in the particular way in which the tetrachord is divided. In the diatonic tetrachord, the fourth is divided into a tone, tone and a semitone - in descending order. In the chromatic tetrachord however, the division proceeds minor third, semitone, semitone - again in descending order. The two types of tetrachord may be compared in fig. 9.1.

Observe that the tetrachord portrayed on the left is a diatonic tetrachord composed of two tones and a semitone. In the chromatic tetrachord on the right however, the pitch of the movable note lichanós has been lowered by a full semitone. Because of this, the scale step between mésē and lichanós is now a tone and a half in size, an interval also referred to as the trihemitone, or minor third. Another, strictly Western interpretation of this scale step is as an augmented second, the interval obtained when a major second is enlarged by a semitone.

Because of this lowering of the lichanós, the scale step between lichanós and parhypátē, which in the diatonic genus is a full tone, now becomes scrunched into a much smaller semitone. This results in a tetrachord composed of scale step sizes of a minor third, semitone and semitone in descending order.

Fig. 9.1: *Comparison of Diatonic and Chromatic Tetrachord*

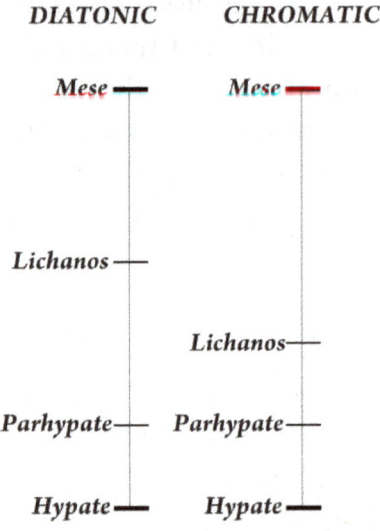

To a certain extent, the chromatic tetrachord represents an extension of the logic that derived a soft diatonic tetrachord from a hard one. This derivation involves lowering the pitch of lichanós. Further lowering leads to such an enlargement of the scale step between mésē and lichanós that it then enters into the perceptual category of an altogether new interval band: the territory of the minor third/augmented second.

Chromatic tetrachords in modern music...

The drooping profile of the ancient Greek chromatic tetrachord can appear unfamiliar to Western musicians. However, considering the three possible species of chromatic tetrachord, as shown in fig. 9.2, enable the chromatic tetrachord to take on a much more familiar apparel.

In the first species, there is a minor third followed by two semitones (in descending order); in the second the minor third appears sandwiched between the two semitones while in the third, the minor third appears at the bottom of the tetrachord.

Fig. 9.2: *The Three Species of Chromatic Tetrachord*

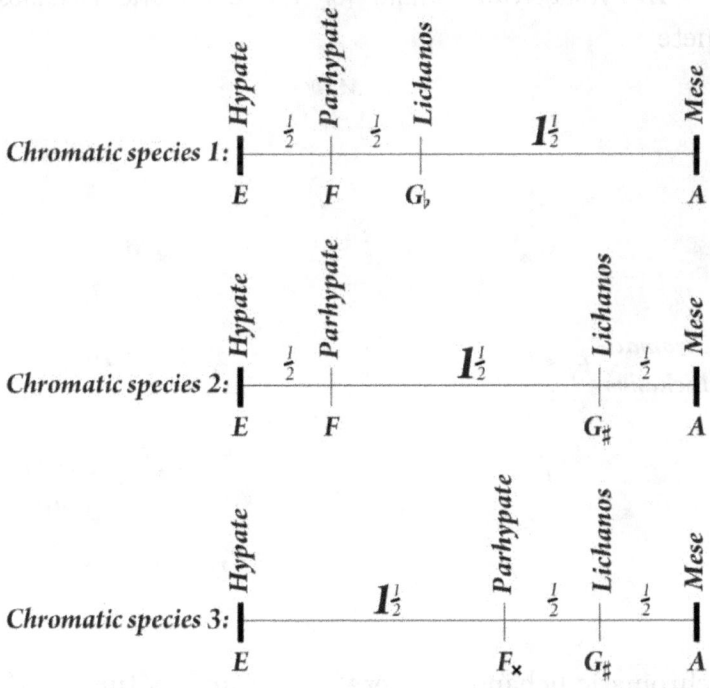

Scales that use this type of tetrachord, particularly the second species shown, are still commonly used in the music of the West, throughout the Middle East, Europe and the Indian subcontinent. Consequently, they are integral features of the modal systems of many cultures.

The harmonic minor mode of Western music uses an ancient Greek chromatic tetrachord, as indeed do many Western so-called synthetic scales, such as the Hungarian minor mode.

The Pythagorean form of the chromatic scale system...

A standard Pythagorean form of chromatic tetrachordal tuning can easily be derived by way of the fifths/fourths up and down principle.

Fig. 9.3: *Pythagorean Tuning for the Chromatic Lichanós and Paranete*

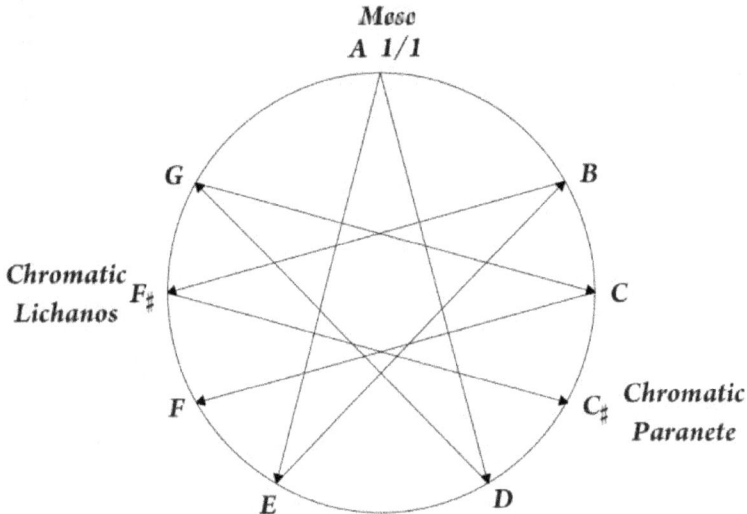

The chromatic lichanós is therefore located by tuning a fourth down (4/3) from paramésē. Tuning up a fifth (3/2) from the chromatic lichanós will then produce the note required for the upper tetrachord; the chromatic paranete (see fig. 9.3). For the lower tetrachord this results in the tuning is illustrated in fig. 9.4. Observe that coming down from mésē (note A), there is a drop of a trihemitone (ratio 32/27) to the chromatic lichanós, note F sharp. From there occur two successive drops of a semitone.

Fig. 9.4: *Ancient Greek Chromatic Tetrachord*

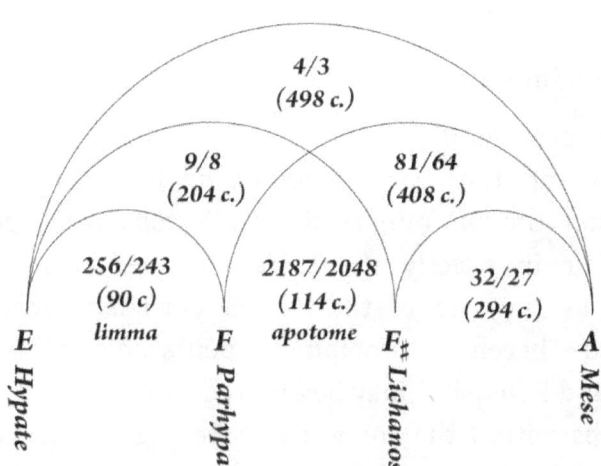

Note that the semitones in this case are of different sizes. This is because the diatonic lichanós has been lowered by a limma (256/243) which is somewhat smaller than half of a tone. A whole tone is 204 cents, while a limma is only 90 cents. This leaves an interval of 114 cents, called an *apotome* (2187/2048), the off-cut left over when a limma is subtracted from a whole tone. When the chromatic tetrachord of fig. 9.4 is duplicated with respect to the fourth between paramésē and nétē, a complete Dorian chromatic scale system in Pythagorean tuning results.

This scale system is illustrated in fig. 9.5. The resulting scale is distinguished by the presence of three main sizes of scale steps: there are two minor third scale steps, one whole tone and four semitone scale steps.

Fig. 9.5: *Dorian Chromatic System in Pythagorean Tuning*

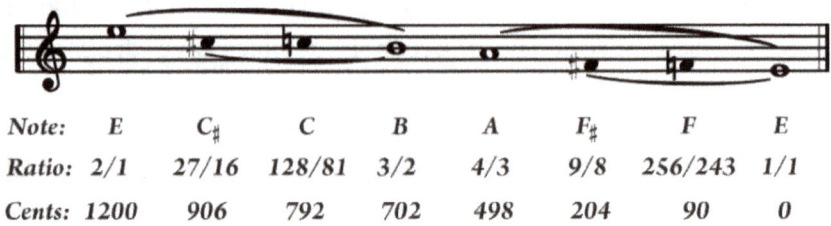

Note:	E	C♯	C	B	A	F♯	F	E
Ratio:	2/1	27/16	128/81	3/2	4/3	9/8	256/243	1/1
Cents:	1200	906	792	702	498	204	90	0

Pentatonic implications of the chromatic genus...

The gaps created by the minor third scale steps are very suggestive of the pentatonic scale. In support of this observation, the two minor third scale steps of the pentatonic scale occur in exactly the same positions relative to one another, as they do in the Dorian chromatic scale system illustrated. Therefore, to obtain the pentatonic scale, the notes C (*Trite*) and F (*hypátē*) may be omitted as shown in fig. 9.6. The scale steps within the inner circle belong to the pentatonic system, while those in the outer circle belong to the ancient Greek chromatic system:

The implied pentatonic character of the ancient Greek chromatic system has been noted by numerous authorities upon the subject.[53] Moreover, it is certainly true that the scale both suggests and embraces the resources of the pentatonic scale, resources that could easily be exploited simply by missing out the requisite notes.

---

[53] An example of this is Curt Sachs who in *The Rise of Music in the Ancient World*, compares certain features of the genera to Asiatic pentatonics. See page 209 in particular.

Fig. 9.6: *Comparison of Pentatonic and Chromatic Systems*

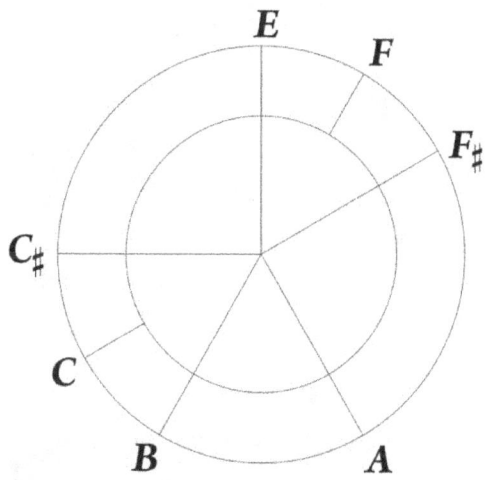

However, could it therefore be argued that the chromatic system as a whole actually derives from an original pentatonic scale? Indeed, was the chromatic system originally simply a pentatonic scale, the intermediate semitones being inserted only much later? Plutarch for example, observed that among the genera, the chromatic was the most ancient. By this, does he therefore mean the pentatonic? If so, then it would mean that the core of the chromatic system is in fact pentatonic, the two extra notes being chromatic auxiliaries.

In support of this argument, is the observation that early lyres had only four or five strings. A method of tuning a five stringed lyre using the traditional fourths/fifths up or down system, would immediately produce a pentatonic scale. The scale illustrated above for example, is definitively implied by the first four fifths, when beginning from the mésē (note A). The first fifth leads to nétē (note E), followed by *paramésē* (note B). The next fifth leads to the chromatic lichanós (note F sharp), after which follows the chromatic paranete (note C sharp). This process is illustrated in fig. 9.7:

Fig. 9.7: *Pentatonic Scale by Way of Tuning Four Fifths up from Mésē*

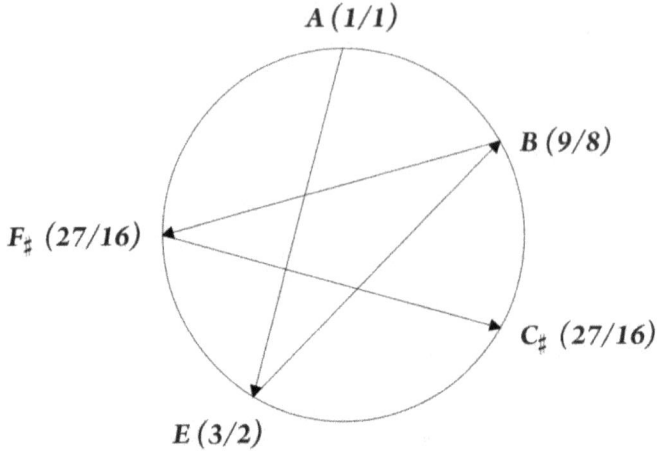

In this context, the pairs of notes C sharp and C, F sharp and F, belonging to the original chromatic system (see fig. 9.5) may be interpreted as being simply major and minor forms of what are essentially the same modal degrees, the sixth in the former case and the second in the latter. As such, the scale comes across as a form of pentatonicism decorated with chromatic inflections, thereby leading to the possibility of using coloristic contrasts between the major and minor forms of those scale degrees.

This however, is only a modern interpretation and there is no evidence to show that this is how ancient Greek musicians thought about the chromatic genus. It appears that the notes C sharp and F sharp signified *different* degrees of the scale, as represented by different strings on the lyre. If so, perhaps it would be more appropriate - in terms of a modern comparison - to think about the minor third steps, not as being of pentatonic origins, but of chromatic origins, representing the appearance of the chromatic interval of the augmented second. In fact, when interpreted as such the integrity of the scale, as a type of heptatonic, rather than pentatonic, is immediately re-established.

If the pentatonic scale was recognized at some time in early Greek music, surely the concept of the trichord would be mentioned somewhere. A pentatonic scale is composed of two such trichords, a hexatonic scale of a trichord and a tetrachord, and a heptatonic scale of two tetrachords. Why weren't trichords ever mentioned by theorists? All that is mentioned is the practice of skipping certain strings. Doing this will inevitably lead to the use of pentatonic structures, although it does not seem that these were perceived as being such. They were standard heptatonic scales from which certain notes had been omitted. Suffice to say, the whole issue of pentatonics in ancient Greek music is a contentious one.

Chromatic octave species...

The inclusion of chromatics (adjacent scale steps of a semitone) may lead to a reconfiguration of the Greater Perfect System, so that it has nineteen notes in total. This would necessitate the inclusion of the chromatic paranétē hyperbolaîon; chromatic paranétē diezeugménon; chromatic lichanós méson and chromatic lichanós hypátē. The result of this is an implied division of the octave into seven main sounds – the notes of the diatonic scale, and two chromatic supplementaries, therefore giving nine notes to the octave. Considering this nine-note system, it comes as a surprise to discover that a complete chromatic scale system was never developed.[54] If such a system had been developed, the ancient Greek scale system would have been that much simpler, for there would have been no need to build the Greater Perfect System on a separate tone for each mode.

As is the case with the diatonic genus, the chromatic genus also

---

[54] A chromatic system was developed, but only in terms of tonos, that is to say the range of 'tones' upon which a Greater Perfect System could be built..

admits of seven particular octave species. These can be worked out by taking each note of the scale as the starting point for a particular species of the chromatic system (fig. 9.8).

Fig. 9.8: *Chromatic Genus Scale Steps*

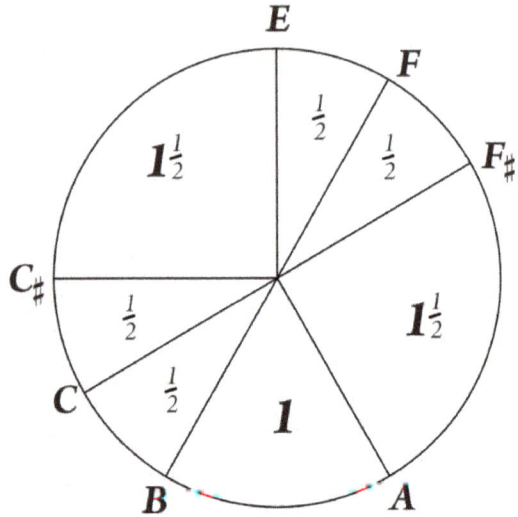

As the scale embraces three scale step sizes – a semitone, whole tone and trihemitone, the possibility arises for a diverse set of resultant modes reflecting the seven octave species of the chromatic scale system. These species are represented as shown in table 8, in which the order of intervals is depicted as descending. These define the sequence of intervals required for each of the seven modes of the chromatic scale, as illustrated in fig. 9.9. All of the modes are here represented as occupying the same octave range from hypátē méson to nétē diezeugménon.

Table 8: *Chromatic Octave Species*

Dorian:	$1\frac{1}{2}$	$\frac{1}{2}$	$\frac{1}{2}$	1	$1\frac{1}{2}$	$\frac{1}{2}$	$\frac{1}{2}$
Phrygian:	$\frac{1}{2}$	$\frac{1}{2}$	1	$1\frac{1}{2}$	$\frac{1}{2}$	$\frac{1}{2}$	$1\frac{1}{2}$
Lydian:	$\frac{1}{2}$	1	$1\frac{1}{2}$	$\frac{1}{2}$	$\frac{1}{2}$	$1\frac{1}{2}$	$\frac{1}{2}$
Mixolydian:	1	$1\frac{1}{2}$	$\frac{1}{2}$	$\frac{1}{2}$	$1\frac{1}{2}$	$\frac{1}{2}$	$\frac{1}{2}$
Hypodorian:	$1\frac{1}{2}$	$\frac{1}{2}$	$\frac{1}{2}$	$1\frac{1}{2}$	$\frac{1}{2}$	$\frac{1}{2}$	1
Hypophrygian:	$\frac{1}{2}$	$\frac{1}{2}$	$1\frac{1}{2}$	$\frac{1}{2}$	$\frac{1}{2}$	1	$1\frac{1}{2}$
Hypolydian:	$\frac{1}{2}$	$1\frac{1}{2}$	$\frac{1}{2}$	$\frac{1}{2}$	1	$1\frac{1}{2}$	$\frac{1}{2}$

When this set of modes are examined as a group (see fig. 9.9 for a portrayal of these), it becomes apparent that some of them have probably not been used for perhaps thousands of years. However, there are two notable exceptions, which are the chromatic Hypodorian and the chromatic Hypophrygian modes, which, strange as it may seem, are well known to modern musicians. For the chromatic Hypophrygian mode is none other than the seven-tone minor blues scale, consisting of a minor pentatonic scale with sharp fourth and seventh. Similarly, the chromatic Hypolydian mode is identical with the seven-tone major blues scale, consisting of the major pentatonic scale with sharp second and flat sixth! We leave the reader to ponder the interesting implications of this.

Fig. 9.9: *The Seven Chromatic Modes*

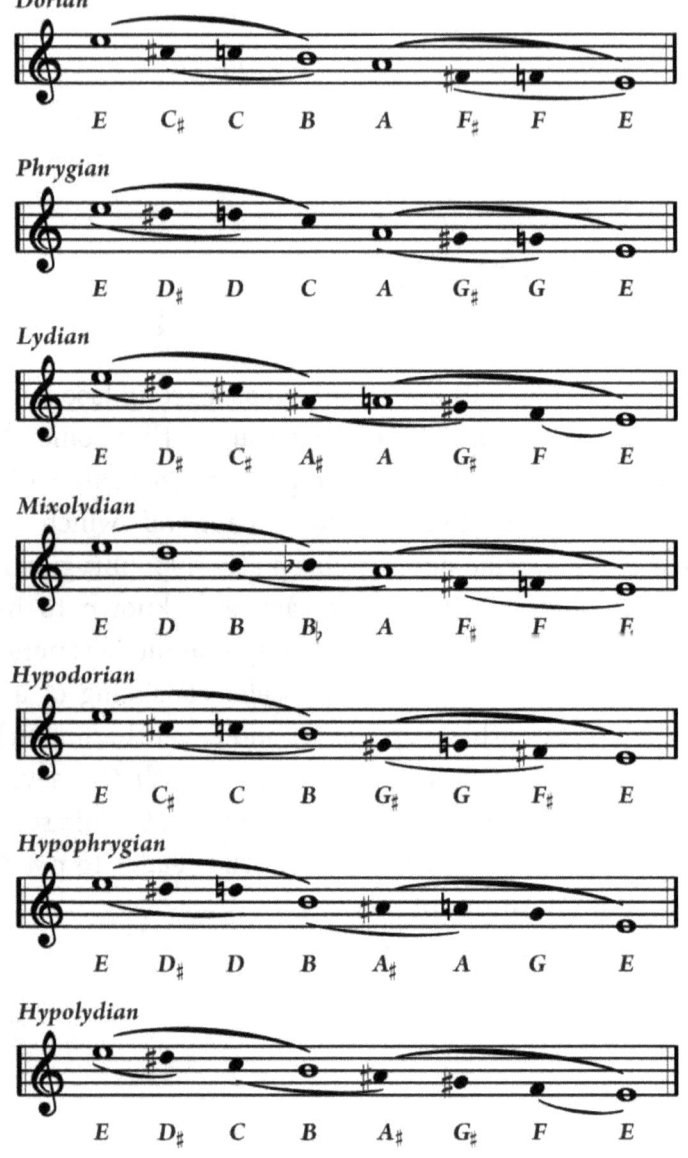

10 Shades of the Chromatic Genus

Like the modes of the diatonic genus, modes of the chromatic genus could also vary in terms of modal shade or colour. The principle arena in which these differences of colour became apparent was with respect to the approach to the *pyknon*, the name given to the now compressed intervallic region between lichanós and hypátē. The word compressed is used, because in the chromatic genus, lichanós is lowered by a semitone, which then brings some three degrees of the scale into a comparatively small range of pitch, the price of that being the increasing size of gap with respect to the mésē.

Aristoxenus' intense chromatic shade...

Aristoxenus' intense chromatic tetrachord is illustrated in fig. 10.1. Observe that the region of the pyknon (between hypátē and lichanós) takes up twelve parts of the tone, while the region between mésē and lichanós takes up eighteen parts. This represents the general qualification for the pyknon i.e. that it is smaller than the gap between mésē and lichanós.

Fig. 10.1: *Aristoxenus' Intense Chromatic Tetrachord*

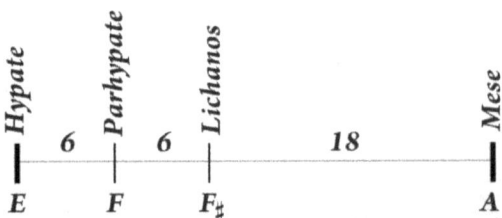

When this structure is duplicated in the upper tetrachord, Aristoxenus' intense chromatic scale system is obtained. See fig. 10.2 for an illustration of this system.

Fig. 10.2: *Aristoxenus' Intense Chromatic Scale*

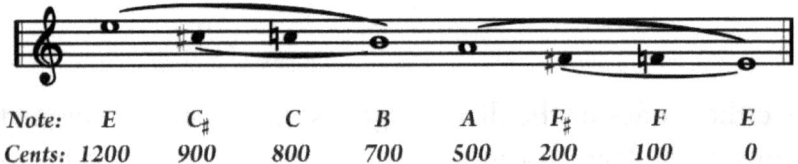

Note:	E	C♯	C	B	A	F♯	F	E
Cents:	1200	900	800	700	500	200	100	0

Now if the intense chromatic is regarded as the standard form for the chromatic tetrachord, to play this tetrachord on a modern instrument the tuning need not be adjusted. This is because Aristoxenus was content to define its terms by unspecified generic intervals of a semitone and a minor third. It therefore proves equivalent to the chromatic system as defined by Pythagorean tuning. However, Aristoxenus also recognized two further shades of chromatic tetrachord: the hemiolic chromatic and the soft chromatic.

Aristoxenus' hemiolic chromatic shade...

In the hemiolic chromatic tetrachord, the minor third scale step between mésē and lichanós is even larger, exceeding the trihemitone by another quarter of a tone. This gives it a magnitude that is half way between a major and a minor third, therefore qualifying it to be a form of neutral third. Because of this enlargement, the pyknon now takes up a region whose magnitude is a neutral tone. Aristoxenus' hemiolic chromatic tetrachord is illustrated in fig. 10.3.

Fig. 10.3: *Aristoxenus Hemiolic Chromatic Tetrachord*

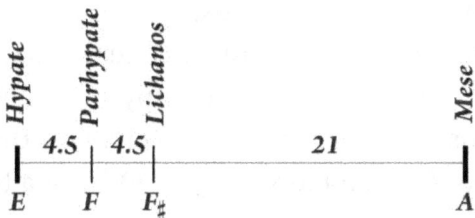

By repeating the tetrachord above the tone of disjunction, the complete Dorian hemiolic chromatic scale system is obtained which appears as shown in Fig. 10.4.

Fig. 10.4: *Aristoxenus' Hemiolic Chromatic Scale System*

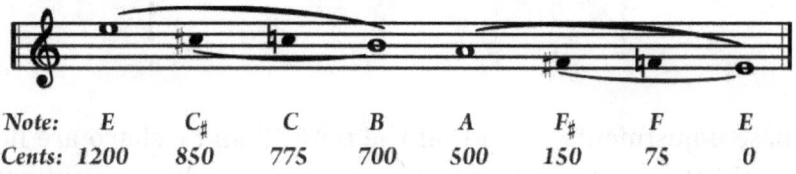

Note:	E	C♯	C	B	A	F♯	F	E
Cents:	1200	850	775	700	500	150	75	0

A quick survey of this system shows that note C sharp (chromatic paranétē) is a quarter tone below its position in the intense chromatic tetrachord, thereby producing an interval whose magnitude is halfway between a major and a minor sixth. It is therefore a type of neutral sixth. Similarly, note F sharp (chromatic lichanós) is similarly displaced, forming an interval of a neutral tone with hypátē. The notes F and C are also flatter than they are in the intense chromatic by an eighth of a tone.

When the positions for the notes of each of the individual modes is calculated, a scale of one-eighth tones is implicated which, in its complete form would therefore have forty-eight notes per octave. As to why Aristoxenus only divided the tone into twelve parts, making it necessary to include calculations to the nearest half-part of one-twelfth is a mystery.

Aristoxenus soft chromatic shade...

A third shade of the chromatic genus recognized by Aristoxenus was the soft chromatic, whose characteristic tetrachord structure is illustrated in fig. 10. 5. Observe that the region of the pyknon is even smaller, now occupying a range of no more than two-thirds of a tone. This in turn enlarges the gap between mésē and lichanós even more, only 2/30ths of a tone short of a complete ditone:

Fig. 10.5: Aristoxenus Soft Chromatic Tetrachord

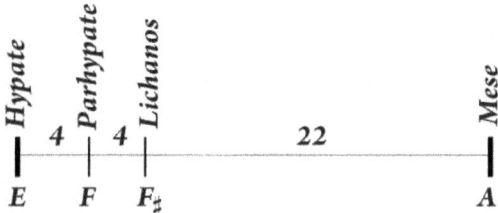

These adjustments mean that the notes C and F sharp are now one-third of a tone lower than their equivalents within the intense chromatic, while notes F and C are similarly a third of a semitone lower. This scale system is shown in fig. 10.6.

Fig. 10.6: Aristoxenus Soft Chromatic System

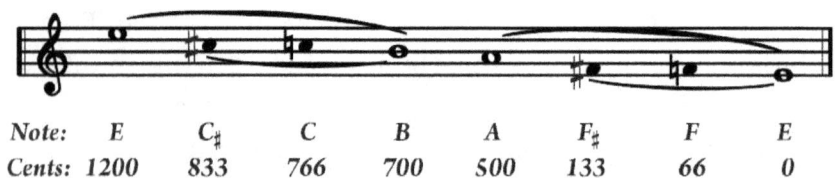

Note:	E	C♯	C	B	A	F♯	F	E
Cents:	1200	833	766	700	500	133	66	0

Aristoxenus soft chromatic shade therefore implies a scale of one-sixth tones which would therefore have thirty-six notes to the octave, many of which would be needed to provide for the positions of the various modes of his soft chromatic shade.

Ptolemy's intense chromatic shade...

Considering the variations in the size of the *pyknon*, as revealed through the different types of chromatic tetrachord formulated by Aristoxenus, it becomes evident that the chromatic genus refers to numerous shades of tetrachord derived from discretely lowering the pitch of the lichanós. This practice can be placed into a clearer perspective by considering ways in which other theorists advocated the tuning of the chromatic genus. Information given by Ptolemy on this subject is again invaluable, especially in terms of the information on note ratios. The advantage of these is that one can more easily place those harmonic relationships that Aristoxenus might have been implying within the terms of his particular system. Ptolemy however, seemed to have recognized only two main shades of the chromatic genus: the intense and the soft chromatic. The intense chromatic tetrachord is as illustrated in fig. 10.7.

Fig. 10.7: Ptolemy's Intense Chromatic Tetrachord

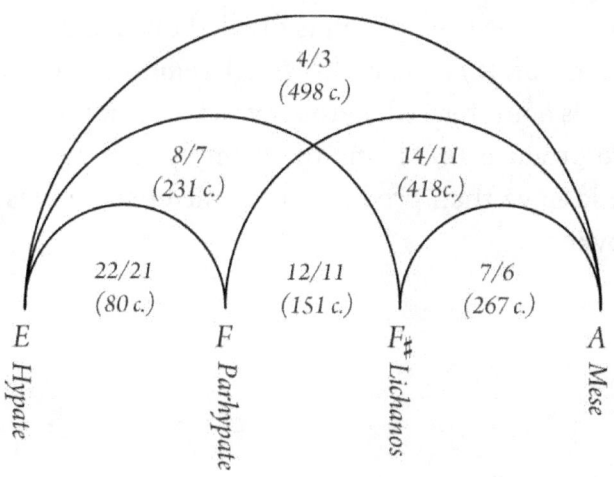

Observe that this divides the perfect fourth (4/3 – 498 c.) between the two septimal epimores 7/6 (267 c.) and 8/7 (231 c.). In this respect, his method was similar to that used for his soft diatonic shade. However, for the intense chromatic, he now reverses their order, placing the larger small septimal minor third 7/6 on top. This offers 7/6 as a substitute for the conventional Pythagorean trihemitone (32/27) between mésē and lichanós.

Ptolemy's next step was to multiply the ratio of the large septimal tone 8/7 by 3 (24/21). Having done so, he then took 22 as a mean, in order to produce 24/22 (12/11) between lichanós and parhypátē and 22/21 between parhypátē and hypátē. The result is that the large septimal tone (8/7) has now been divided unequally between the neutral tone of ratio 12/11 and the small semitone of ratio 22/21.

When this tetrachord is repeated above the tone of disjunction, Ptolemy's intense chromatic system is obtained (fig. 10.8). An examination of the cents measurements for the notes of this scale, show that Ptolemy is giving himself considerable leeway in terms of his methodology for dividing the pyknon. All forms of Aristoxenus' chromatic tetrachord divided the pyknon equally into two halves, whereas in the case of Ptolemy's intense chromatic the pyknon is divided unequally between the neutral tone of 12/11 and the small semitone of 22/21. Here perhaps it is a mystery why Ptolemy did not simply multiply 8/7 by two to produce 16/14, and then simply took 15 as the mean. This would have then produced the pair of semitones required for the pyknon.

Fig. 10.8: *Ptolemy Intense Chromatic System*

Note:	E	C♯	C	B	A	F♯	F	E
Ratio:	2/1	12/7	11/7	3/2	4/3	8/7	22/21	0
Cents:	1200	933	782	702	498	231	80	0

The scale step sizes for Ptolemy's intense chromatic system are shown in fig. 10.9. From these, the various modes of Ptolemy's intense diatonic shade can be worked out.

Fig. 10.9: *Scale Step Sizes in Ptolemy's Intense Chromatic System*

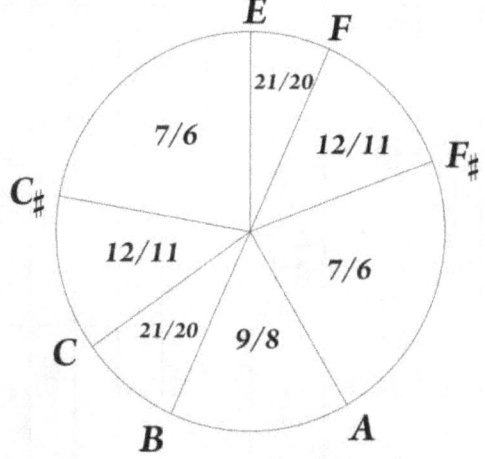

When the various positions for the notes of these modes are calculated the result is a scale of some twenty seven notes, which is shown in fig. 10.10.

In this particular scale, ratios using the prime number five are conspicuously absent, the emphasis instead being placed on ratios involving the prime numbers seven and eleven.

Fig. 10.10: *Tuning for the Seven Modes in Ptolemy's Intense Chromatic Shade*

	Note	Ratio	Cents	Dorian	Phrygian	Lydian	Mixolydian	Hypodorian	Hypophrygian	Hypolydian
1	E	2/1	1200	●	●	●	●	●	●	●
27	D♯	21/11	1120		●					●
26	D♯	11/6	1049	●				●		
25	D	16/9	996							
24	D	7/4	969		●		●	●		
23	C♯	12/7	933	●				●		
22	C♯	56/33	916		●					
21	C	18/11	853							●
20	C	11/7	782	●				●		
19	C	14/9	765		●					
18	B	32/21	729				●			
17	B	3/2	702	●				●	●	●
16	A♯	45/28	649			●				
15	A♯	63/44	622							●
14	A♯	88/63	578				●			
13	A♯	11/8	551						●	
12	A	4/3	498	●	●	●	●			
11	A	21/16	471						●	
10	G♯	9/7	435				●			
9	G♯	14/11	418			●				●
8	G	11/9	347	●						
7	G	33/28	284					●		
6	G	7/6	267	●				●		
5	F♯	8/7	231	●		●				
4	F♯	9/8	204					●		
3	F	12/11	151		●					●
2	F	22/21	80	●		●				
1	E	1/1	0	●	●	●	●	●	●	●

Ptolemy's soft chromatic shade...

Ptolemy also offers his version of the soft chromatic tetrachord which is shown in fig. 1011. This reverts to the epimoric minor third (6/5) for the mésē-lichanós scale step, while the minor tone pyknon is divided between the large septimal semitone of 15/14 and Archytas preferred small septimal semitone of 28/27.

To arrive at this tetrachord Ptolemy probably began by multiplying the ratio of the perfect fourth by 3, to produce 12:9. He then took the mean 10 to establish the upper limit for the pyknon. Then, multiplying the ratio of the interval bounding the pyknon (10/9) by 3, he obtained 30/27. Taking twenty-eight as the mean, he thereby obtained a division of the pyknon into the small septimal semitone of 28/27 and the large septimal semitone of 15/14.

As a sequence of whole numbers, this tetrachord would read 27:28:30:35. This produces a tetrachord very similar in its tuning for the tetrachord he offers for Archytas' chromatic, the major difference being the size of the pyknon which, in Archytas' chromatic tetrachord is a major tone (9/8) while in Ptolemy's tetrachord the pyknon is a minor tone (10/9).

Like his intense chromatic tetrachord, Ptolemy's soft chromatic tetrachord does not attempt to divide the pyknon into two equal halves on a par with Aristoxenus' shades of the chromatic tetrachord. Indeed, he could have easily multiplied the ratio of the pyknon (10/9) by two to produce 20/18 and then have taken 19 as the mean. This would have produced a more balanced division of the pyknon into two halves.

Fig. 10.11: *Ptolemy Soft Chromatic Tetrachord*

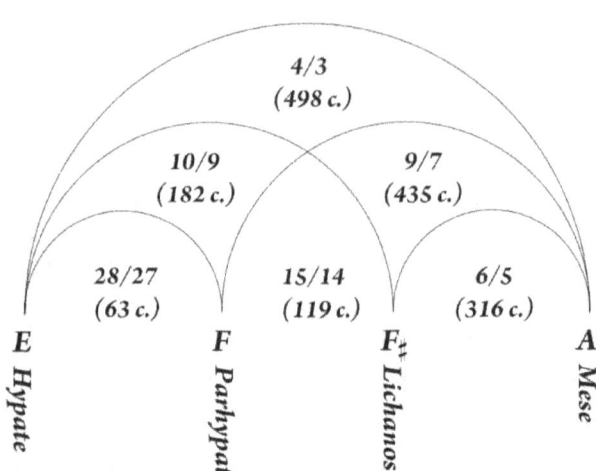

When Ptolemy's soft chromatic tetrachord is duplicated in the upper tetrachord the scale as shown in fig. 10.12 appears.

Fig. 10.12: *Ptolemy Soft Chromatic System*

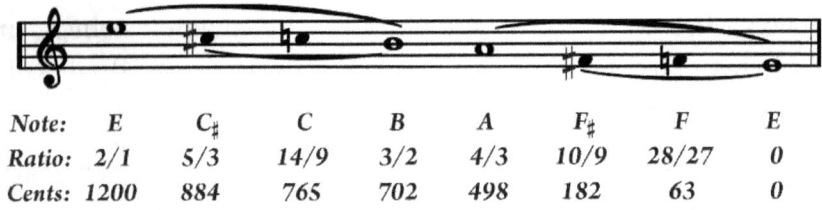

Note:	E	C♯	C	B	A	F♯	F	E
Ratio:	2/1	5/3	14/9	3/2	4/3	10/9	28/27	0
Cents:	1200	884	765	702	498	182	63	0

Observe the way in which Ptolemy has integrated the powers of three prime numbers in his tuning for this scale. There is the prime number three as represented by the fixed tones A and B, the prime number five as represented by the pair of notes C sharp and F sharp, and the prime number seven as represented by the notes F and C. When the particular tuning for the seven modes that this implies is worked out, the result is a scale of some twenty-seven notes which is shown in fig. 10. 13.

Microtonality in Ancient Greek Music

Fig. 10.13: *Tuning for the Seven Modes in Ptolemy's Soft Chromatic Shade*

	Note	Ratio	Cents	Dorian	Phrygian	Lydian	Mixolydian	Hypodorian	Hypophrygian	Hypolydian
1	E	2/1	1200	●	●	●	●	●	●	●
27	D♯	27/14	1137			●				●
26	D♯	28/15	1081		●				●	
25	D	9/5	1018		●				●	
24	D	16/9	996				●			
23	C♯	12/7	933			●				
22	C♯	5/3	884	●				●		
21	C	45/28	821							●
20	C	8/5	814		●					
19	C	14/9	765	●				●		
18	B	3/2	702	●				●	●	
17	B	40/27	680				●			
16	A♯	81/56	639							●
15	A♯	10/7	617			●				
14	A♯	7/5	583						●	
13	A♯	112/81	561				●			
12	A	27/20	520						●	
11	A	4/3	498	●	●	●	●			
10	G♯	9/7	435			●				●
9	G♯	5/4	386					●		
8	G♯	56/45	379		●					
7	G	6/5	316		●			●		
6	G	7/6	267					●		
5	F♯	9/8	204					●		
4	F♯	10/9	182	●			●			
3	F	15/14	119			●				●
2	F	28/27	63	●			●			
1	E	1/1	0	●	●	●	●	●	●	●

Alternative chromatic tunings...

In his list of the chromatic shades Ptolemy presents Archytas' chromatic tetrachord. This preserves some sense of continuity with Archytas' diatonic tetrachord, for both the small septimal semitone between hypátē and parhypátē (28/27 - 63 cents) as well as the septimal interval 9/7 (231 cents) between mésē and parhypátē are retained. This leads to the employment of what is very nearly a neutral tone (243/224 - 141 cents) between parhypátē and lichanós. Archytas chromatic tetrachord is as illustrated in Fig. 10.14:

Fig. 10.14: *Archytas' Chromatic Tetrachord*

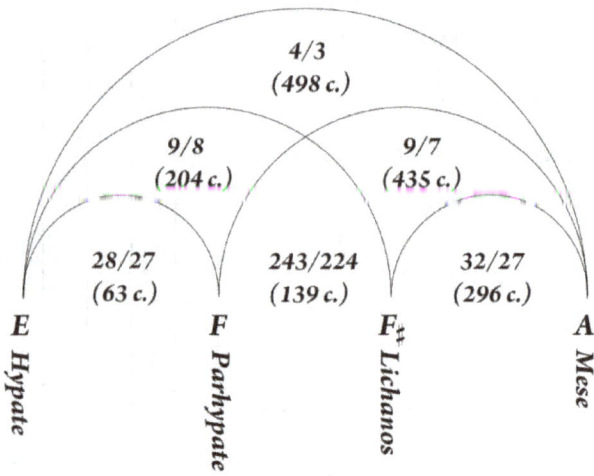

The resulting Dorian chromatic scale tuning is as appears in Fig. 10.15. This shows that Ptolemy's soft chromatic system is virtually identical, except for the harmonic major sixth (5/3 - 884 cents) which Ptolemy uses in preference to Archytas Pythagorean major sixth (27/16 - 906 cents) and the minor tone (10/9 - 182 cents) which Ptolemy employs in favor of the major tone (9/8 - 204 cents) of Archytas.

Fig. 10.15: *Archytas' Chromatic Tuning*

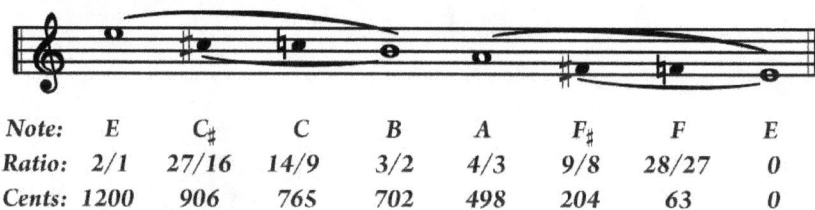

Note:	E	C♯	C	B	A	F♯	F	E
Ratio:	2/1	27/16	14/9	3/2	4/3	9/8	28/27	0
Cents:	1200	906	765	702	498	204	63	0

Ptolemy also lists a chromatic tuning, which he attributes to Didymus. In Didymus chromatic tuning, an extension of the mathematical logic applied to his diatonic tuning is apparent. Simple ratios involving the prime number five are employed where possible, the pyknon being divided unequally between the major semitone of ratio 16/15, and the minor semitone of ratio 25/24. Like Ptolemy's soft diatonic tetrachord, the pyknon in this case therefore spans a minor tone of ratio 10/9. (Fig. 10.16).

Fig. 10.16: *Didymus Chromatic Tetrachord*

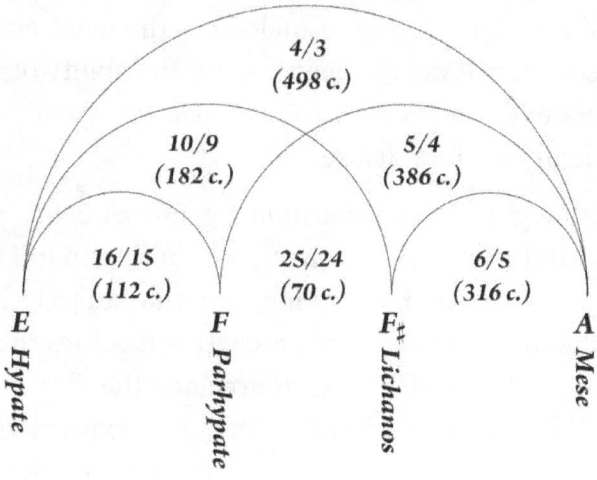

11 The Enharmonic Genus

Although regarded by Aristoxenus to have been the noblest of all styles,[55] the enharmonic genus ostensibly involved the use of microtones in a melodic context. This therefore necessitated the use of a certain degree of melodic refinement and subtlety which it seems, eventually went beyond the ability of audiences to appreciate. Consequently, the enharmonic genus seemed to have gradually fell into disuse.

Plutarch thought of the enharmonic genus as being one of the most beautiful of the three genera, attributing to it a grave and solemn character. In his writings on the subject, he clearly laments the loss of those finer perceptive faculties that enabled audiences to distinguish and appreciate the fine microtonal intervals that represented one of the chief expressive features

---

[55] Aristoxenus, *Elements of Harmony*, 23.

of the enharmonic genus.[56]

The enharmonic pyknon...

In terms of its basic profile, the enharmonic tetrachord was characterized by a pyknon of even greater density than the chromatic genus. This can be appreciated through reference to Aristoxenus' model of the enharmonic genus as shown in fig. 11.1.

Fig. 11.1: *Aristoxenus Enharmonic Genus*

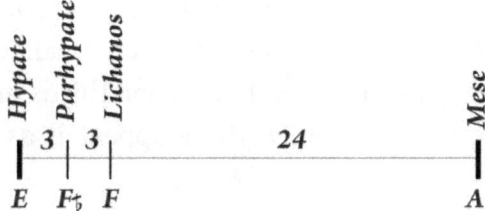

The pitch of the chromatic lichanós has been lowered even further than in the chromatic genus, thereby expanding the breadth of the scale step between mésē and lichanós into the range of a ditone (the breadth of two whole tones or a major third). This leads to a further shrinking of the breadth of the pyknon into the range of a semitone, which is now divided between two quarter tones, resulting in a tetrachord whose scale steps in descending order are major third, quarter-tone, quarter-tone.

A complete Dorian enharmonic scale system, obtained by duplicating the enharmonic tetrachord above the tone of disjunction, would therefore appear as follows. The symbol of a flat with a diagonal stroke through it signifies a half-flat, that is

---

[56] Plutarch, *Op. Cit.*, section 38.

to say the lowering of a note by half of a semitone. See fig. 11.2.

Fig. 11.2: *The Dorian Enharmonic Scale System*

Note:	E	C	C♭	B	A	F	F♭	E
Cents:	1200	800	750	700	500	100	50	0

The seven enharmonic modes...

From the characteristic pattern of intervals as they appear in the Dorian enharmonic system the various octave species of the enharmonic scale can now be considered, all of which will consist of four quarter tones, two major thirds and one whole tone step. The order in which these appear is as shown in fig. 11.3.

Fig 11.3: *Scale Step Sizes in the Enharmonic Scale System*

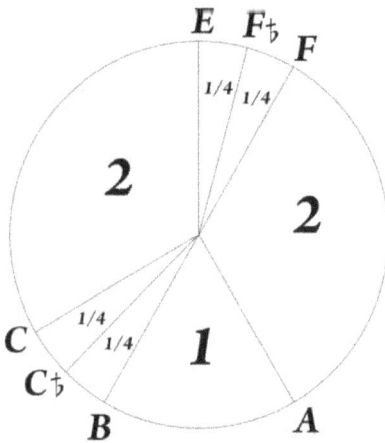

Representing the enharmonic scale visually in this fashion, highlights the curious juxtaposition of minute microtonal scale steps on the one hand, combined with what appear to be large ditonal leaps on the other. This gives the enharmonic scale a unique profile, one that is clearly a far cry from the relative evenness and balance of the diatonic scale with its much more familiar juxtaposition of tone and semitone.

The seven octave species of the enharmonic scale can be worked out from fig. 11.3 by taking each of the seven points on the circumference of the circle as the beginning point for a particular species. These are as shown in table 9, in which the scale steps are presented in their descending order. These in their turn provide the substantive basis for configuring the seven modes of the enharmonic scale within the same octave range.

Table 9: *Octave Species of the Enharmonic Scale:*

Dorian:	2	$\frac{1}{4}$	$\frac{1}{4}$	1	2	$\frac{1}{4}$	$\frac{1}{4}$
Phrygian:	$\frac{1}{4}$	$\frac{1}{4}$	1	2	$\frac{1}{4}$	$\frac{1}{4}$	2
Lydian:	$\frac{1}{4}$	1	2	$\frac{1}{4}$	$\frac{1}{4}$	2	$\frac{1}{4}$
Mixolydian:	1	2	$\frac{1}{4}$	$\frac{1}{4}$	2	$\frac{1}{4}$	$\frac{1}{4}$
Hypodorian:	2	$\frac{1}{4}$	$\frac{1}{4}$	2	$\frac{1}{4}$	$\frac{1}{4}$	1
Hypophrygian:	$\frac{1}{4}$	$\frac{1}{4}$	2	$\frac{1}{4}$	$\frac{1}{4}$	1	2
Hypolydian:	$\frac{1}{4}$	2	$\frac{1}{4}$	$\frac{1}{4}$	1	2	$\frac{1}{4}$

Using the profile provided for by the seven octave species, the seven modes of the enharmonic genus, as represented within the octave range from nétē down to hypátē can be worked out. These are as shown in fig. 11.5.

The enharmonic genus and major third pentatonic scales...

When the seven modes of the enharmonic genus are examined, taking particular care to play them on a specially tuned musical instrument, the enharmonic scale looks, sounds and even seems to behave like a major third pentatonic scale that has been adorned with a couple of quartertone auxiliaries. The relationship between the two scale systems – major third pentatonic and ancient Greek enharmonic is as shown in fig. 11.4, where the inner circle shows the major third pentatonic scale, the outer circle the enharmonic scale.

Fig. 11.4: *Comparison of Major Third Pentatonic and Enharmonic Scale Systems*

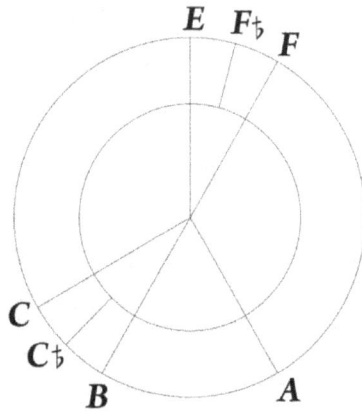

Comparing the two scales in this fashion is clearly enough to create the impression that the enharmonic scale was no more than a basic pentatonic structure that used two microtonal decorative notes. Plutarch perhaps confirms these suspicions when he recounts the origins of the enharmonic scale, which were often attributed to the legendary aulos player Olympus. Apparently, in a passage involving descending diatonic movement, 'he passed several times directly from paramésē and mésē to parhypátē; omitting the lichanós; and being greatly pleased with the beauty of the effect produced by this series of sounds he constructed upon it a new system the principle of which was the invariable omission of the lichanós'[57]

---

[57] Plutarch, *Op. Cit.*, Sect. 11.

Fig. 11.5: *The Seven Enharmonic Modes in Staff Notation*

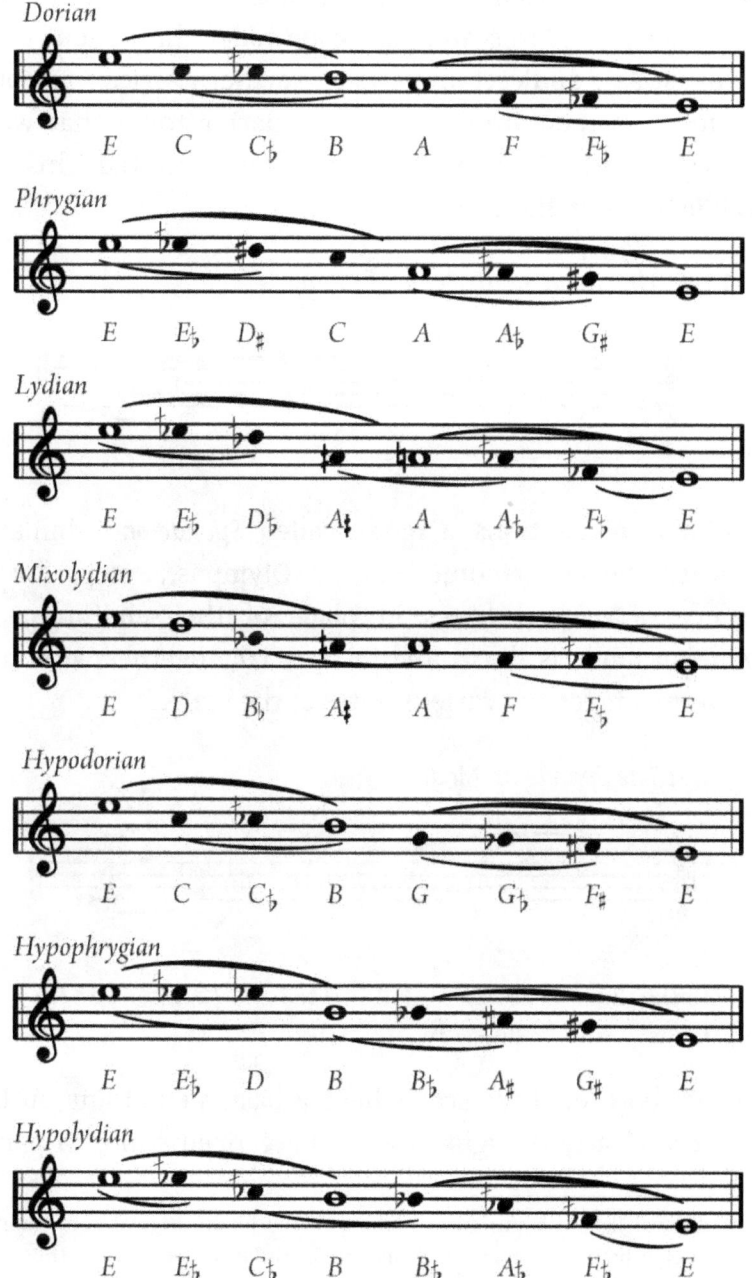

Applying a similar gap as that mentioned by Plutarch, to the upper tetrachord would produce a major third pentatonic scale of a similar profile to scales used even today throughout Japan, South-East Asia and certain parts of Northern Africa. To obtain this form of pentatonic scale the quarter tones that would otherwise split the two semitones are simply omitted. This scale is as illustrated in fig. 11.6.

Fig. 11.6: *The Enharmonic Scale of Olympus*[58]

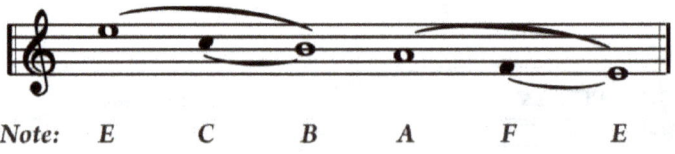

Note: E   C   B   A   F   E

Plutarch also mentions a mode called *Spondeion*[59] similar in profile to the enharmonic scale of Olympus, except for the presence of neutral tones in place of the semitones. The Spondeion mode is illustrated in fig. 11.7, together with cents measurements for the various notes of the scale.

Fig. 11.7: *The Spondeion Mode*

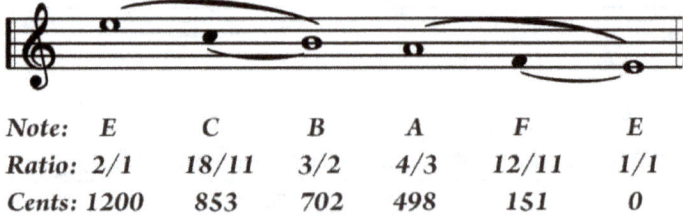

Note:	E	C	B	A	F	E
Ratio:	2/1	18/11	3/2	4/3	12/11	1/1
Cents:	1200	853	702	498	151	0

Although both of these scales have a basic pentatonic outline, they were clearly thought of as being gapped scales. A part of

---

[58] In traditional Japanese music this scale, as based on an original koto tuning, is called Kumoi Joshi. In Ethiopian traditional music it is known as Ambassel (minor).

[59] See R. P. Winnington-Ingram (1928), *The Spondeion Scale*

the mystery surrounding these is the circumstances surrounding the splitting of the semitone of the original enharmonic scale into quarter tones, something that was certainly practically feasible on an instrument such as the aulos through half-covering certain finger holes. Moreover, although tuning the strings of the lyre to quartertones presents certain problems, these are not insurmountable seeing that it is only necessary to find a mid-point between two strings tuned a semitone apart. First perhaps, the player would tune the pentatonic core as represented by the enharmonic scale of Olympus, leaving parhypátē and trítē to be tuned last.

Ptolemy's enharmonic tuning...

One of the surprising features surrounding the study of the enharmonic genus is that, even though it seemed to have had only one shade, not one of the theorists seemed to have agreed on the best way to tune that shade. Indeed, we will now examine some of the different ways in which various theorists recommended the tuning of the enharmonic scale, beginning first of all with Claudio Ptolemy's approach to the problem.

Beginning with the bare fourth, Ptolemy first addresses the tuning of the ditone, for which he selects the sweet sounding epimoric major third of ratio 5/4. This leaves him with a pyknon spanning a diatonic semitone of ratio 16/15, an interval no doubt commendable by virtue of its super particular ratio. This threefold division of the fourth is very similar to that which Ptolemy employs in his intense diatonic tetrachord, the difference being that lichanós now takes the place of parhypátē as the lower note of the major third.

Ptolemy then addresses himself to the splitting of the pyknon, which he does by multiplying the ratio of the diatonic semitone by three to produce 48/45. He then takes 46 as the mean, to produce a large quartertone of 24/23 (74 cents) between lichanós and parhypátē, and a small quartertone of 46/45 (38 c.) between parhypátē and hypátē. As such, Ptolemy makes no efforts whatsoever, to try to split the semitone into two equal halves as Aristoxenus does.

Fig. 11.8: *Ptolemy's Enharmonic Tetrachord*

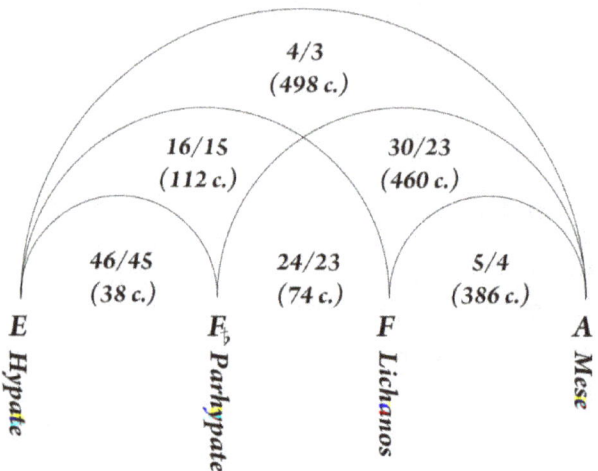

Duplicating this tetrachord above the tone of disjunction, we obtain the Dorian enharmonic scale system which is as shown in fig. 11.9

Fig. 11.9: *Ptolemy's Enharmonic Scale System*

Note:	E	C	C♭	B	A	F	F♭	E
Ratio:	2/1	8/5	23/15	3/2	4/3	16/15	46/45	0
Cents:	1200	814	740	702	498	112	38	0

When assessing Ptolemy' enharmonic scale system, the minute size of the enharmonic diesis between hypátē and parhypátē and paramésē and trítē is very conspicuous. Here one is caused to wonder why Ptolemy did not opt for the same solution as Didymus, which was to multiply the ratio of 16/15 by two to produce 32/30 and then divide the semitone more or less equally between the quartertone dieses 32/31 and 31/30. This tuning of Didymus is illustrated in fig. 11.10.

Fig. 11.10: *Didymus Enharmonic System*

Note:	E	C	C♯	B	A	F	F♯	E
Ratio:	2/1	8/5	48/31	3/2	4/3	16/15	32/31	0
Cents:	1200	814	757	702	498	112	55	0

In Archytas' enharmonic tetrachord, a similar approach is taken in the main details, the only difference being in the way in which he split the 16/15 pyknon, which he does between the septimal dieses 36/35 (49 c.) and 28/27 (63 c.). It is interesting to observe that Archytas therefore used the septimal interval 28/27 in all three of his genera. The reasons for this are not clear, especially as, in the diatonic genus, this small septimal semitone takes the place of a full diatonic semitone and in the enharmonic genus a relatively minute quartertone. The onus for all three of Archytas' genera therefore lies on the particular tuning of the lichanós. See Fig. 11.11 for an illustration of Archytas enharmonic system.

Fig. 11.11: *Archytas Enharmonic System*

Note:	E	C	C♯	B	A	F	F♯	E
Ratio:	2/1	8/5	14/9	3/2	4/3	16/15	28/27	0
Cents:	1200	814	765	702	498	112	63	0

The only exception to the use of the 5/4 ditone and 16/15 semitone is Eratosthenes, who evidently began with an enharmonic tetrachord in Pythagorean tuning. However, as the ratios involved were so cumbersome, he sought out the nearest equivalents in terms of simpler ratios. His ditone thus has a ratio of 19/15, only 1 cent short of an 81/64 Pythagorean ditone of 408 cents. Similarly Eratosthenes' limma pyknon is given a ratio of 20/19 (89 cents), again 1 cent short of the Pythagorean limma of 256/243. He then divides his limma more or less into two equal halves in the way of 39/38 (45 cents) and 40/39 (44 cents). Eratosthenes enharmonic system is illustrated in fig. 11.12.

Fig. 11.12: *Eratosthenes Enharmonic System*

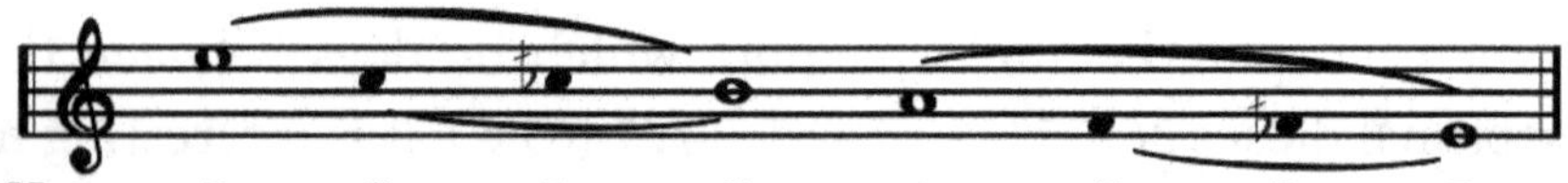

Note:	E	C	C♯	B	A	F	F♭	E
Ratio:	2/1	30/19	60/39	3/2	4/3	20/19	40/39	0
Cents:	1200	790	746	702	498	88	44	0

It is interesting to see that not one of the theorists agrees as to how to tune an enharmonic tetrachord, especially when it comes to the tuning of the quartertones. As these could not be appreciated by audiences in the first place, makes all of these various efforts to arrive at a logical and feasible tuning the enharmonic scale rather pointless. Is it possible for the human ear to distinguish between quartertones of 46/45, 40/39, 32/31, and 28/27? Moreover, for that matter, why did Archytas include a quartertone in all of his genera, even the diatonic?

12 Reviewing the Ancient Enharmonic System

Through our thumbnail sketch of the three genera so far, we have seen that ancient Greek musicians enjoyed access to a far wider range of scalar resources than are available to today's musicians. Examining these resources however, seems to yield nothing but a recipe for confusion. Where did the three genera come from? And for that matter, where did the shades themselves come from? The entire system seems to have arisen in the first place from some kind of root plan or foundation which now seems to be missing. The result is a mass of fragments with no real indication of their ultimate source.

Another missing element seems to be the grounding of certain scale systems within that corpus of musical experience that Aristoxenus so wisely alluded to. How for example, does the enharmonic genus relate to that corpus of experience? Because if the enharmonic genus is real, rather than some kind of abstraction, it may be assumed that it would connect at some point with that corpus of experience, which in turn would enable us to know how, or at least from what, it arose. Yet there seems to be some kind of disconnect that has taken place between the domain of that experience on the one hand and the theory of the enharmonic genus on the other. This tends to give the impression, mistaken or otherwise, that the enharmonic genus is no more than a theoretical abstraction, a problem toy of the philosophers that never had any practical value.

The problem seems to be particularly acute with the enharmonic genus, because at least as far as the chromatic genus is concerned, there is sufficient evidence to show that the scales still find a practical use in the music of numerous different cultures, even to this day. The modes of Byzantine chant are a good example of this, in which numerous modes are even today recognized as belonging to the line of the ancient Greek chromatic genus. In this sense therefore, there is still a connection between musical experience and theory which gives to that scale system a practical usage and relevance.

In terms of the enharmonic scale however, it is difficult at first to find any practice, anywhere in the world, that seems somehow to conform with, validate or corroborate what ancient Greek theorists had to say about the enharmonic genus. There are of course certain similarities that emerge between the different musical traditions that at least invite tentative comparisons.

Curt Sachs' comparison with traditional Japanese major third pentatonic scales is a good example of this, where numerous different types of pentatonic scale are used, some of which are minor third pentatonic scales based on traditional Chinese models; some of which are major third pentatonic scales, which seem to be uniquely Japanese and others of which offer a delightful mixture of major and minor thirds. The similarity of the Japanese major third variety of pentatonic scale with the enharmonic scale of Olympus is indeed striking, and there is no doubt that there is a powerful affinity between these scale systems, even if this only comes down to similarities in their structural constitution.

There are also valid comparisons to be drawn with similar types of pentatonic scales as used in the traditional music of Vietnam, for there we find the use of not only a mix of major and minor third pentatonic scales, but also the highly expressive use of microtonal inflections of certain degrees of the scale. A good example of this is the Vietnamese vong cô mode, a mixed major and minor third pentatonic scale in which the major third and sixth are deliberately lowered by a fraction of a tone, while the fourth is deliberately raised slightly. These microtonal alterations of certain degrees of the scale, created by exerting a certain pressure on the strings of the dàn nguyêt lute, are used as expressive gestures calculated to enhance the feeling of nostalgia typical of the songs that use this mode.[60]

This practice certainly seems to share some affinities with the enharmonic genus of ancient Greece. However these are only external similarities which do not go to show or explain the root out of which the enharmonic genus actually grew. Indeed, all of these comparisons are based on the assumption that the enharmonic scale is basically a pentatonic scale that has been dressed up with microtones – whereas this may not actually be the case.

---

[60] See Dr Phong, Th. Nguyen, *Restructuring the Fixed Pitches of the Vietnamese Dan Nguyêt Lute: A Modification Necessitated by the Modal System*, p.61 – 62,

Pythagorean cyclic method of scale division...

When endeavoring to ascertain the root of the enharmonic genus, one line of investigation that might be productively explored is what is loosely termed Pythagorean intonation. However, these terms tend to belie the fact that originally, this was not so much a system of intonation, but a system of scale generation based on the mathematical properties of two geometric progressions, the first an expression of the powers of the prime number two, the second the powers of the prime number three.

Students of Plato may recognize these progressions as expressed through the form of the Platonic Lambda, as shown in fig. 12.1, where they then become symbolic of the process whereby the various partitions of the world soul were generated, as explained in rather cryptic fashion by Plato in the Timaeus.

Fig. 12.1: *Plato's Lambda*

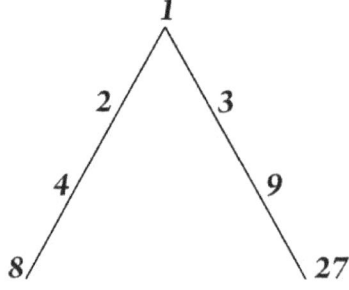

The application of these numbers to the process of scale division has already in part been discussed in chapter three, where various divisions of the monochord were considered. As viewed in these terms, the number 1 at the apex of Plato's Lambda signifies the undivided open string of the monochord. This represents the generator of the two proportions: the number two and its various powers signifying the halving of the string whereby the octave is obtained, the number three and its powers signifying the division of the string into three parts whereby the interval of the perfect fifth is obtained. These two proportions, in their subsequent interactions, generate a complete musical cosmos; a series of increasingly complex musical scales, which we will now consider.

The first staging post is reached by the first two fifths rising up from note A. These produce note E of ratio 3/2 and then note B of ratio 9/8, thereby establishing at the very outset, the basic structure that divides the empty octave space into two skeletal tetrachords separated by a whole tone, as shown in fig. 12.2.

Fig. 12.2: *The Fixed Tones Generated by the First Two Fifths*

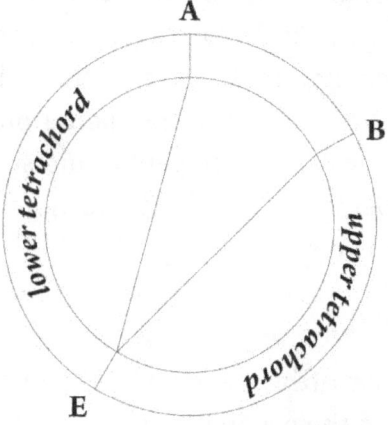

In this way, the three fixed tones are generated right at the very outset, awaiting only the arrival of the movable notes whose positions will be filled in by subsequent members of the cycle of fifths. Therefore it is perhaps significant that the addition of a further two fifths leads to a division of the upper and lower tetrachords into two trichords, composed of a whole tone (9/8) and a trihemitone (32/27). This process is illustrated in fig. 12.3. While these trichords do not seem to have been recognized by Greek theorists, they were certainly recognized by virtually every other world musical culture.

Fig. 12.3: *Pentatonic Scale Resulting from First Four Fifths*

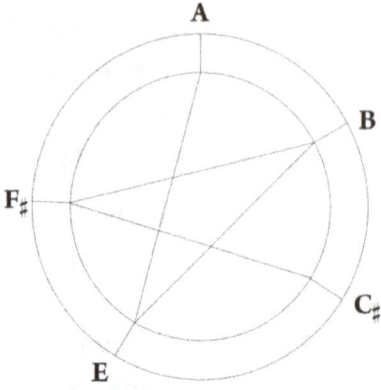

The pair of trichords so formed yields the pentatonic scale in its more traditional minor third form, a scale which was probably the first musical scale ever to have been developed and used by humanity. Taking each note in its turn to be the respective tonic, generates the five pentatonic modes, among which can be found the major pentatonic scale (tonic note A) and the minor pentatonic scale (tonic note F sharp) so well known to Western musicians today.

The diatonic scale...

When a two further fifths are added, they divide the two minor thirds belonging to the original pentatonic scale into a tone and a semitone each, thereby producing the familiar pattern of tones and semitones recognizable as belonging to the diatonic scale. This scale is illustrated in fig. 12.4. Here therefore, we have the seven harmoniai of ancient Greek music, derived from the process of taking each note of this scale to be the prospective tonic. These correspond to the seven diatonic modes that are also well known to musicians today.

Fig. 12.4: *Diatonic Scale Produced by Six Fifths*

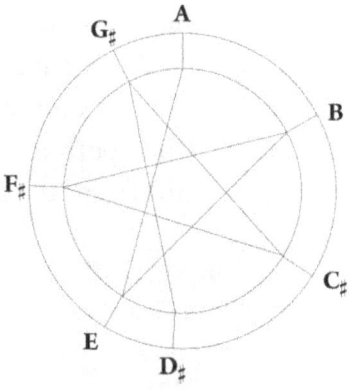

Subsequent fifths then place themselves in such a way as to subdivide the remaining whole tones into two semitones. The next two fifths for example, divide the whole tones between notes A and B; E and F sharp as shown in fig. 12.5. This produces a scale of nine notes that includes the seven notes of the original diatonic scale, plus the two chromatic auxiliaries as used in the ancient Greek chromatic genus. When these auxiliaries are used as substitutes for two of the degrees of the original diatonic scale, the ancient Greek chromatic scale of seven notes results.

Fig. 12.5: *Nine-note Scale Produced by First Eighth Fifths*

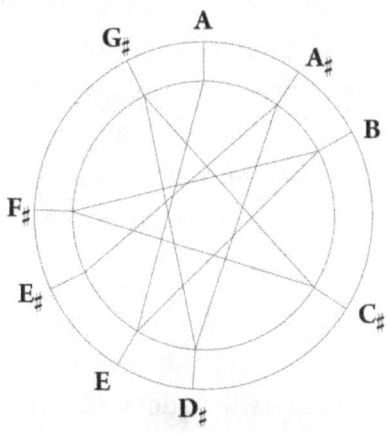

The Pythagorean form of chromatic scale...

By the eleventh fifth, all of the whole tones belonging to the original diatonic scale have now been subdivided to produce a pair of semitones in each case, the one small (the limma of 256/243) and the other large (the apotome of ratio 2187/2048). The result is the Pythagorean form of chromatic scale as illustrated in fig. 12.6.

Fig. 12.6: *Pythagorean Chromatic Scale*

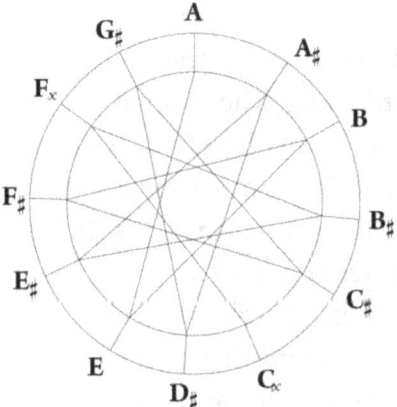

A point of interest that arises from this, is that the chromatic notes thus generated, do not manifest perceptually as being altogether new degrees of the scale. On the contrary, they manifest as alternative positions for the various degrees of the scale that have already been established by the first six fifths. In other words, they tend to manifest as alternative positions for the movable notes, the usefulness of which arises from the fact that they are all directly invoked in the process of modal expression.

Any scale system built on semitones in this fashion is of necessity chromatic. As such, the first twelve members of the cycle of fifths embrace two orders of scalar possibility: the diatonic whose scalar focus is the whole tone, and the chromatic whose scalar focus is the semitone. In terms of ancient Greek scales, these orders of possibility are represented respectively, by the diatonic genus on the one hand, and the chromatic genus on the other. However, there is as yet, no intimation of the shades, only the intimation of basic Pythagorean forms of both diatonic and chromatic genera.

However logic would suggest that if the implications for two genera are already present within the unfolding but potentially infinite sequence of perfect fifths, then the implications for more advanced or subsequent genera, such as the enharmonic, probably lie beyond the bounds of the twelfth fifth.

However, the twelfth fifth clearly represents a powerful demarcation point, for its trajectory brings it into extremely close orbit with the frequency of the generator with which the cycle was started (1/1). However, rather than meeting up with the generator, the twelfth fifth slightly overshoots the mark by a Pythagorean comma (ratio 531441/524288 – 22 cents), as portrayed in fig. 12.7. An arrow indicates exactly where the twelfth fifth falls.

Fig. 12.7: *Pythagorean Comma Resulting from Twelfth Fifth*

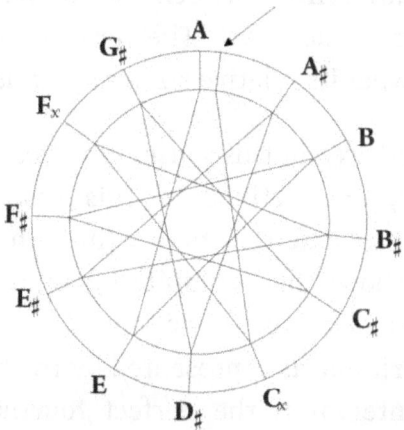

The twelfth fifth therefore represents the point where the chromatic circle is closed. However, in closing one circle of possibility another circle opens up, for the sequence of fifths then continues through yet another cycle of twelve, but this time each new fifth places itself a Pythagorean comma higher than the previous set of twelve fifths. Subsequent fifths thereafter all place themselves yet another comma higher, and so the process continues up until the fifty-second fifth, where all of the semitones belonging to the original chromatic scale have now become subdivided into commas, four in the case of the limma and five in the case of the apotome.

The fifty-second fifth in this case, represents the point of closure of yet another circle of possibility. This is the enharmonic circle which deals in the possibility for finer levels of expression than the semitone. Hence one of the characteristic features of the enharmonic circle is the division of the semitone into various fractional parts.

In terms of the cycle of fifths, its own objectively unfolding mathematical structure naturally implies a division of each semitone into four parts for the minor or small semitone (the limma), and five parts for the major or large semitone (the apotome). The difference between the limma and apotome in this respect, is one such part. The term for such a fractional part, no matter what its relative size, is *enharmonic diesis*.

The scale of fifty-three in this sense, provides an example of an *enharmonic scale*, one defined in this case by the natural sequence of fifths as it spirals its way through the octave space. This in its turn shows that within the bounds of the first fifty-two fifths, there are five basic orders or levels of scalar possibility: the tritonic as represented by the three fixed tones, whose salient interval is the perfect fourth; the pentatonic which the Greeks seem to have passed over, whose salient interval is the minor third; the diatonic whose salient interval is the whole tone; the chromatic whose salient interval is the semitone and finally the enharmonic whose salient interval is the enharmonic diesis. These may be cast up as a fourfold enclosure, in which one possibility lies nestled within the other, as illustrated in fig. 12.8.

Fig. 12.8: *Fourfold Enclosure of the Cycle of Fifths*

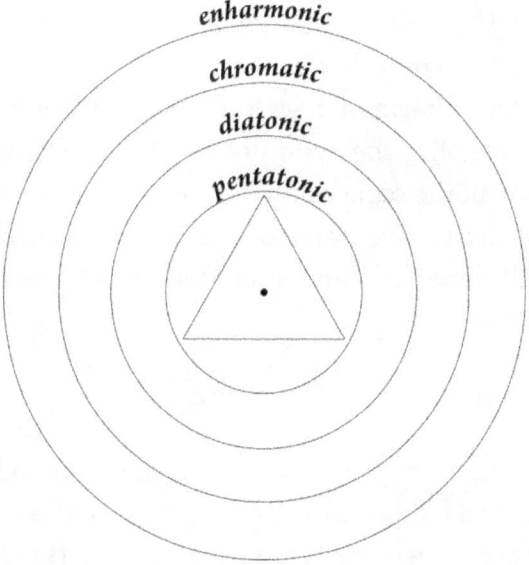

This diagram encapsulates the following information:

- The central dot signifies the number one, the generator, the open string of the monochord, the fundamental, the central point from which the cycle of fifths is considered to be generated.
- The triangle signifies the three fixed tones that provide the balanced framework and foundation for all subsequent scale formations.

- The four circles represent the various orders of scalar possibility so far discussed.

If we accept that the diatonic embraces and subsumes the pentatonic possibility, then it can be asserted that ancient Greek music made effective use of all of these circles of possibility, as demonstrated principally by the genera, that is to say the diatonic, chromatic and enharmonic, whose level of activity corresponded directly with the circles indicated.

Observe that the enharmonic circle of possibility begins with the twelfth fifth where the semitone is first divided to yield a microtone. An enharmonic scale may therefore be defined as any scale that splits the semitones of the chromatic scale. As such an enharmonic scale can have any number of notes beyond the range of the twelve notes of the chromatic scale. The need for these will depend upon which degrees of the scale require enharmonic support.

The enharmonic scale of Safi al Din...

Inevitably, our comprehension of the possibility of the enharmonic scale is affected by the fact that Western music does not proceed beyond the bounds of the third circle. This means that, unlike the diatonic and chromatic genera, there are no equivalent models in the traditional canon of Western music with which it is possible to relate the enharmonic genus of ancient Greek music.

There are however, appropriate models in the music of other cultures that did not necessarily reject the resources of the enharmonic scale. A good example of this is the scale formulated by the thirteenth century Arabic theorist Safi al-Din al-Urmawi in his music treatise the Kitab al-Adwar. This scale is based on a sequence of sixteen fifths, which means that it has seventeen notes to the octave. See Table 10 for an illustration of this scale.

Table 10: *Safi al-Din's Enharmonic Scale*

Note ratio	Derivation	Cents
1/1	*Fundamental*	0
256/243	5th *fourth*	90
65536/59049	10th *fourth*	180
9/8	2nd *fifth*	204
32/27	3rd *fourth*	294
8192/6561	8th *fourth*	384
81/64	4th *fifth*	408
4/3	1st *fourth*	498
1024/729	6th *fourth*	588
262144/177147	11th *fourth*	678
3/2	1st *fifth*	702
128/81	4th *fourth*	792
32768/19683	9th *fourth*	882
27/16	3rd *fifth*	906
16/9	2nd *fourth*	996
4096/2187	7th *fourth*	1086
1048576/531441	12th *fourth*	1176
2/1	*Octave*	1200

For a long time in the West, it was commonly assumed that this scale used one-third tones, it being taken more or less for granted that it was a division of the octave space into seventeen parts. However, it is more appropriately understood as being an enharmonic scale in which the positions of certain notes could be altered slightly, thereby offering the facility for distinguishing between scale step sizes of a major and minor tone and semitone, that is to say the highly expressive use of *enharmonic distinctions* between tones.

This facility in its turn, thereby enabled a finer level of modal expression capable of expressing subtle colours that are beyond the bounds of the chromatic scale alone. Consequently, of the seventeen notes of this scale there are twelve belonging to the original Pythagorean form of the chromatic scale plus five extra notes, which provide alternative positions for certain of the semitones.

When different positions of the same semitone are being implied, as they clearly are in Safi al-Din's scale, these are essentially *enharmonic* distinctions of tone (i.e. involving an appreciation of intervals smaller than a semitone). This can be appreciated by representing the seventeen note enharmonic scale in the form of an illustration, which can be seen in fig. 12.9.

Fig. 12.9: *Safi al Din's Enharmonic Scale*

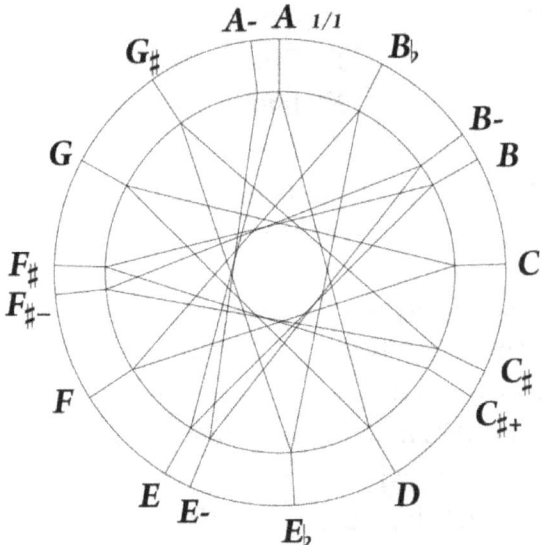

Assuming A to be the modal tonic, notice that the whole tone above the tonic occurs in two forms – note B, which is the major tone, and note B-, which is the Pythagorean equivalent of the minor tone. Similarly, the major third degree also occurs in two forms, note C sharp plus which is the Pythagorean ditone, and note C sharp which is the Pythagorean equivalent of the harmonic major third. These different positions for the *same semitone* in each case (separated as they are by a single enharmonic diesis), are invoked by the use of different modes. In one mode, note C sharp is required, while in another note C sharp plus.

Now although in this case enharmonic dieses are not being used as successive scale steps, as they seemed to have been in the ancient Greek enharmonic genus, the sphere of operation is nonetheless still enharmonic, simply because the system of modes that are used are entirely dependent upon the presence of the enharmonic diesis.

This in its turn, shows quite clearly that the ancient Greek shades could only have arisen in the first place, on the enharmonic level, for the simple reason that differentiation by shade depends entirely upon recognition and use of the enharmonic diesis. Indeed, this is all that distinguishes between say, the intense diatonic and the soft diatonic. In the former case there is use of the regular whole tone, while in the latter, use is made of a whole tone that is larger than the regular tone by one diesis.

The point of discussing the cycle of fifths as a method of scale generation therefore, lies only in the fact that it shows that progression through the diatonic, chromatic and enharmonic circles is automatically implied by the winding progression of the spiral of fifths through the octave. Accordingly, there are three possible levels of expression belonging to these domains. The main feature of the diatonic is the tone; of the chromatic, the semitone and of the enharmonic, the diesis i.e. use of intervals smaller than the semitone. Consequently, these three may be regarded as being perfectly natural orders of musical expression and there is nothing obscure or esoteric, about any of them.

Subtleties of intonation…

If the spiral of fifths provides a useful clue to unraveling some of the mysteries of the enharmonic genus, another clue arises from the process of listening carefully to the intonation of singers, in particular those who sing in traditional styles of folk music. Here, especially when singing unaccompanied, I have often heard the use of many, what often seem to be quite instinctive but highly expressive and subtle variations of pitch. These are so common in fact that they are clearly integral to various folk styles of singing.

To notate these subtle variations of pitch would be extremely difficult using Western notation. Indeed, in the past, due to a general pre-occupation with the rigid semitones of equal temperament, these subtleties of intonation have often been simply ignored, forgotten about or even treated as an aberration and 'corrected'. What is being ignored or corrected in this case, is clearly a perfectly natural use of the enharmonic circle of possibility.

This observation in its turn, might help to mend any schism between practice and theory that made of the enharmonic level of expression something that was essentially quite remote, abstract, and obscure. Suspecting this to be the case, I asked a folk singer to sing the enharmonic scale of Olympus for me– but in doing so to feel free to use any subtle changes of pitch as quite naturally occurred to them. Once the singer had found their way around the scale and felt relaxed singing, they instinctively began to raise the second and sixth notes by about a quarter of a tone when rising, and lower those same notes by about a quarter of a tone when descending. Asking the reasons for this, I was told that these subtle twists of pitch were felt to enhance the felt connection between the notes of the scale. This practice just 'felt right' in other words.

Perhaps this is the true enharmonic scale, alive and as fresh today as it probably was in ancient Greece. When rising, hypátē and trítē are omitted, when falling paranétē and lichanós are omitted. Daniélou mentions a similar practice with respect to the Indian classical music mode *Gunkali*, which has an identical profile to the enharmonic scale of Olympus. In this context he observed that classical Indian singers and performers tend to use a large semitone on ascent and a smaller one on descent. He felt this to be an expressive gesture deliberately employed to enhance the feeling of the mode, which he describes as 'that dash towards joy which turns back into melancholy'.[61] The ancient Greek enharmonic scale in other words.

Coming back to the experiment just described, in another rendition of the same scale, the singer also felt the urge to sing a different version in which the second and sixth were raised in such a way as to create a neutral tone with the first and the fifth. This form of expression of the scale sounded not only very natural to the ear, but it also became apparent that by inflecting the notes of the scale in this way, that the singer was intoning the ancient Greek *Spondeion* mode that Plutarch mentioned. Moreover, this is from no more than observing the practice of a singer who has no knowledge of ancient Greek music or scales whatsoever, no classical training in the performance of microtonal music, but simply a natural feeling to follow the

---

[61] Alain Daniélou, *Introduction to the Study of Musical Scales*, p. 104.

inclination of the voice with respect to what felt right.

This experiment proved to me something that I had suspected, which is that the enharmonic scale may have been the foundation for a subtle, but entirely natural practice. It is well known that in Western music, many folk melodies have been disfigured beyond all recognition by forcing them into the straightjacket of Western notation, with its necessary reduction of the flexible and elastic world of the tone into rigid semitone blocks.

That ancient Greek scales may have been intoned differently depending upon their ascent or descent is perhaps implied by Aristides Quintilianus when he observed, "a descent of three incomposite dieses was called eklysis, an ascent of the same interval spondaeiasmos, and an ascent of five dieses, ekbole. These were given names as modification of intervals because of the scarcity of their use".[62]

If it were not regular practice to employ subtly different intonations of the same scale degree depending upon whether the scale was rising or falling, why would there be different names for exactly the same interval? Why was an ascent of five dieses called an ekbole, but the same interval in descent had no name? This certainly indicates that the practice Daniélou mentions, might also have been used in ancient Greek music.

Modern use of enharmonic scales...

In this context, the enharmonic scale amounts to no more than the recognition of the expressive use of intervals finer than the semitone, an expressive resource that classical composers and musicians long ago sacrificed in favor of the ability to modulate freely between different keys belonging to the diatonic genus.

---

[62] Mathiesen, *Op. Cit*, p.538..

As such, the enharmonic genus undoubtedly shows a concern for a certain refinement of expression that is distinctly at odds with the values of traditional Western music. For this reason perhaps, the enharmonic genus is often viewed as being something extraordinary, exotic, eclectic or requiring years of practice to master.

However, the use of those finer distinctions of tone characteristic of the enharmonic genus is not at all unusual or exotic for the music of those cultures that, throughout their history, have developed a keen sense for the various parameters of modal expression. Here can be discerned clear references to the enharmonic domain, both in terms of their fundamental approach to matters of modality and more especially, in the use of foundation scales that go beyond the limiting chromatic world of the semitone.

Obvious examples of this are the Hindu scale of twenty-two shrutis, or indeed, the current foundation scale of Arabic modal music that has twenty-four notes. These are examples of *enharmonic scales*, and in both of the cases just mentioned, subsume both the resources of the chromatic *and* diatonic scales. Once this has been recognized, it becomes apparent that in ancient Greece, there might originally have been just one scale system – the enharmonic - of which the chromatic and diatonic, together with all of the shades, were originally subsets.

The validation for this view perhaps lies in the use of the neutral tone, a use which is still as alive today as it clearly was in the music of ancient Greece. The difference between the neutral tone and the regular whole tone is an enharmonic diesis. As such, when singers utilize neutral tones they are in effect, employing an enharmonic distinction between tones. Therefore, it is absurd to say that the ear cannot detect the use of quartertones, for it can easily detect the audible difference in effect between a whole tone and a neutral tone. That difference is an enharmonic difference and it operates at the level of an enharmonic scale. In this context, use of the neutral tone, or indeed, any other neutral interval, counts as proof that the enharmonic scale system never passed into obscurity.

Consequently, any theoretical system, Western or otherwise, that recognizes use of the neutral tone, must of necessity base itself, not on a chromatic scale as a first principle, but on an enharmonic scale that accounts for these finer enharmonic distinctions. Otherwise, the practices of a live, vital music are being ignored in favor of a theory that does not properly account for actual practice. Here, wherever musicians or singers 'split' the semitone, there the enharmonic is to be found. Clearly this applies across the board, irrespective of whether the performer is an Irish folk singer, a kora player of Western Africa, an Arabic oud player or indeed, a player of the ancient Greek lyre or aulos.

The scale of enharmonic dieses...

That there was originally an enharmonic scale system is confirmed by Plutarch, who observed that 'in their treatise we find no direction given on the use of the diatonic genus or the chromatic, but of the enharmonic alone: and none of the systems in this genus except that which is called the diapason.'[63] He also observes that 'with respect also to the manner of dividing the tones or the other genera they were not agreed; but are almost unanimous in maintaining that there is but one species of the enharmonic'.[64]

---

[63] Plutarch, *Op. Cit.*, Section 34. This observation by Plutarch is based on earlier statements by Aristoxenus.

[64] Ibid.

Plutarch even makes known the foundations for this ancient enharmonic system.[65] Speaking of the incompatibility of the enharmonic diesis with symphony on the behalf of critics of the enharmonic genus, he argues that 'they forget that they ought, for the same reason, to discard from practice the third, fifth and seventh intervals, which consist respectively of three, five and seven dieses.'[66]

Plutarch is clearly referring here to a scale of enharmonic dieses, as well as scale step intervals composed of three dieses – the neutral second, five dieses – the maximum tone, and seven dieses – the neutral third. He then goes on to report that 'indeed, all the uneven intervals (or those which contain the smallest diesis an uneven number of times) ought on the same ground be rejected, since none of them can be used in symphony.'[67]

The allusion to a scale of enharmonic dieses becomes even more explicit here, the quartertone steps which he mentions consisting of an uneven number of dieses, the semitone steps an even number. He concludes with the observation that 'it is in fact a necessary result of their doctrine that no divisions of the scale are applicable to practice except those in which the intervals are expressed by even numbers: the intense diatonic for instance, and the tonic chromatic'.[68]

In these statements Plutarch is thinking in terms of, and expressing himself through the idea of a basic structure of an

---

[65] Plutarch, *Op. Cit.*, Section 38.

[66] Ibid..

[67] Ibid..

[68] Ibid..

enharmonic scale composed of at least twenty-four quarter-tones, of which the even numbered members form the scale of semitones. Upon these even numbers all of the degrees of both the intense diatonic and tonic chromatic scales do indeed rest. Moreover, Plutarch even speaks of a scale of intervallic classification based on quarter-tone units, in which an interval of three-quarters of a tone for example, is called a third interval; an interval of five-quarters of a tone a fifth interval, and so on.

However, it would be mistaken to view the enharmonic scale as being simply a division of the octave into twenty-four equal quartertones. The enharmonic scale clearly signifies the various points in the octave where a clearly perceptible modal expression *may* occur. Such expressions would usually be represented by a note ratio, which means that the enharmonic diesis itself is infinitely flexible in terms of its expressive magnitude.

However, when these points of modal expression *are* anticipated in an extended scale system, the theory of the three genera then collapses, for they then become no more than subsets of a single genus, which is the enharmonic. In other words, once recognized, the enharmonic scale subsumes all of the other circles of possibility. From this standpoint therefore, there is only one genus, which is the enharmonic, and this genus represents the fundamental root from which all of the other scale systems, including the shades, actually come from.

This can easily be demonstrated by dividing the tetrachord into ten enharmonic dieses. Once this has been accomplished it becomes apparent that there are only thirty-six possible ways of dividing that fourth into three intervals such as to create a potentially usable tetrachord. Each of these are expressible in numerals signifying the number of dieses in each instance.

Therefore for example, the diatonic tetrachord composed of two tones and a semitone is expressible as 4, 4 and 2. See fig. 12.10.

Fig. 12.10: *Diatonic Tetrachord of 4, 4, and 2 Dieses*

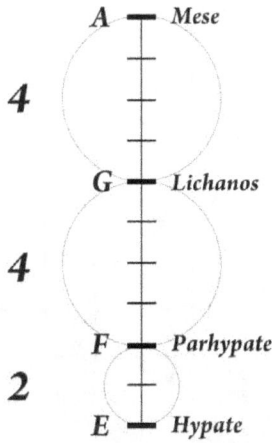

Now among those thirty-six ways of dividing the perfect fourth, there are many cases of species repetition, that is to say repeats of what is the same tetrachordal division, where species of the tetrachord are taken into account. Therefore, three such repeating instances are 4, 4 and 2; 4, 2 and 4 and 2, 4 and 4. These refer to the three possible species of diatonic tetrachord. Now when all of these repetitions by species are eliminated, the result is that there are only twelve unique divisions of the tetrachord, given the enharmonic diesis as the basic unit. These are shown in fig 12.11.

Now at this stage, this represents no more than the use of mathematics to reveal potentialities. As such, this process has no apparent musical relevance. However, by going through this process of simple enumeration, all of the genera and shades spoken of by the ancient writers on Greek music are present and accounted for. Furthermore, they all seem to be derivative from what was clearly once a comprehensive platform for ancient Greek musical scales, which is a scale of enharmonic dieses.

Fig. 12.11: *Twelve Divisions of the Tetrachord in a Fourth of Ten Dieses*

X	X	X								X	118
X	X		X							X	127
X		X	X							X	217
X	X			X						X	136
X		X		X						X	226
X			X	X						X	316
X	X				X					X	145
X		X			X					X	235
X			X		X					X	325
X	X					X				X	154
X		X				X				X	244
X			X			X				X	334

When these twelve possible tetrachordal divisions are examined the existence of a certain conditionality emerges, one that explains not only the constitution of the three genera, but also the source for the modern myth of the pentatonic origins of ancient Greek scales. The clue to this lies in the gap between mésē and lichanós, the first division of the tetrachord when viewed as a descending progression of four notes.

- If that gap is a tone, leaving a minor third left over, the genus has to be diatonic because of necessity the minor third must then be split two ways. Accordingly, the conditionality for the diatonic genus is expressible as a trichord using the notes A G E.

- If the gap is a minor third, with a tone left over, the genus has to be chromatic because of necessity, the tone must then be split into two semitones. Accordingly, the conditionality for the diatonic genus is expressible as a trichord using notes A F# E.
- If the gap is a major third, with a semitone left over, then the genus has to be enharmonic, for the simple reason that the remaining semitone must be split by two quarter-tones. Accordingly, the conditionality for the diatonic genus is expressible as a trichord using notes A F E.

As such, the genera assume certain conditionalities that in themselves lead to the formulation of scales. Consequently, when a scale conforms to the conditionality of the diatonic i.e. there is a whole tone between mésē and lichanós, then this scale belongs to the diatonic genus. The three units designative of these conditionalities are therefore trichords, since only two qualifying factors are needed. The first is the mésē – lichanós gap, the second is the gap left over – between lichanós and hypátē. The three trichordal units are therefore as shown in fig. 12.12:

Fig. 12.12: *Trichordal Conditionalities of the Genera*

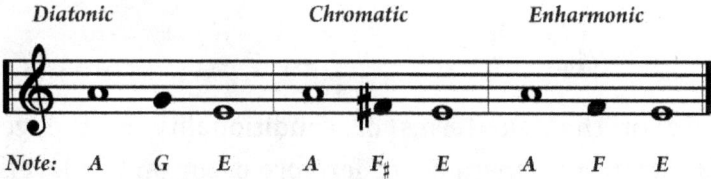

Sach's comparison of ancient Greek scales with Japanese models of the pentatonic scale is therefore based on no more than the coincidence of these trichordal units with the three possible trichords used by Japanese major and minor third pentatonic scales. The difference between these and the scales of ancient Greece is that in the case of Japanese music, a pentatonic intentionality may have been present, while in the music of ancient Greece, any pentatonicism that occurred was probably an incidental result of the deliberate employment of a certain subset of the heptatonic scale i.e. through the practice of skipping certain notes as an expressive gesture.

Fig 12.13: *Five Types of Tetrachord*

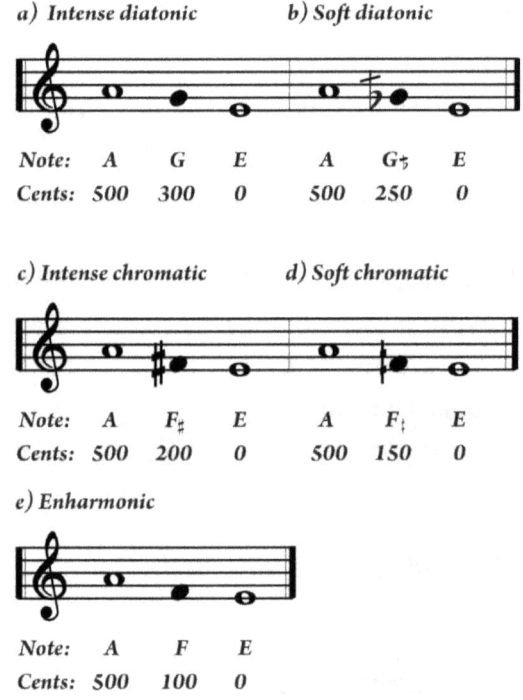

Because of the two terms of conditionality of the genera, variations in the genera may therefore occur on two levels. The first is variation in the magnitude of the first interval between mésē and lichanós. Where the whole tone is four dieses in magnitude (fig. 12.13a) the shade is intense diatonic. Where the whole tone is five dieses in magnitude the shade is *soft diatonic* (Fig. 12.13b).

Similarly, the minor third of the chromatic genus can clearly be either six or seven dieses in magnitude. The six diesis minor third is the regular trihemitone of the *intense chromatic* (fig. 12.13c) while the seven diesis minor third is the neutral third of the *soft chromatic* (fig. 12.13d).

Finally, the major third is of one size only, a size of eight diesis (fig. 12.13e). Consequently, there is only one enharmonic division, which is 8, 1 and 1. This explains Plutarch's statement that 'all are almost unanimous in maintaining that there is but one species of the enharmonic'.[69]

The second level of variation of the shades stems from the different ways in which the remaining interval can be divided. In terms of the *intense diatonic*, the remaining six dieses may be split in three ways:

a) 4 and 2,
b) 5 and 1,
c) 3 and 3.

a) is the *intense diatonic* which counts as the standard or regular shade for the diatonic scale, consisting of two tones and a semitone. In this context the semitone tends to vary between the minor form (90 cents) and the major form (112 cents). Similarly, the tone can be either major (204 cents), or minor (182 cents).

b) is Archytas diatonic, termed *diatonic with soft chromatic diesis* by Aristoxenus and *whole tone diatonic* by Ptolemy. In this tetrachord the regular whole tone is followed by the maximum tone, which is ordinarily given a ratio of 8/7, and a measurement of five dieses as opposed to the four dieses of the regular whole tone. This leaves a single diesis at the bottom of

---

[69] Plutarch. *Op. Cit.*, Sect. 38.

the tetrachord.

c) is Ptolemy's *equable diatonic* in which the minor third of six dieses is divided into two more or less equal neutral tones consisting of three dieses each.

In terms of the *soft diatonic*, where the tone is five dieses in magnitude, the remaining five dieses may be split in two different ways:

    a) 4 and 1
    b) 3 and 2

a) is Ptolemy's *intense chromatic* which has therefore been wrongly classified. Clearly this is a species of soft diatonic tetrachord.

b) is both Aristoxenus' and Ptolemy's *soft diatonic* shade.

In terms of the *intense chromatic* where the minor third is six dieses in magnitude, the remaining four parts may be split in two ways:

    a) 2 and 2
    b) 3 and 1

a) is the regular or standard form of the chromatic tetrachord as implied by Pythagorean tuning. This consists of a minor third of six dieses at the top with two semitones of two dieses each at the bottom of the tetrachord. It therefore corresponds to Aristoxenus *intense chromatic* and Didymus' chromatic tetrachord.

Tetrachord b) is Ptolemy's wrongly classified *soft chromatic* or Archytas' chromatic in which the semitones are replaced by a neutral tone of three dieses and a single quarter-tone diesis.

In terms of the *soft chromatic* where the minor third is seven dieses in magnitude, the remaining 3 parts may be split in only one way, that is between two and one diesis. This division implies the ancient *spondeion* mode mentioned by Plutarch, although surprisingly, hardly any of the theorists offer examples of this type of tetrachord, except perhaps for Aristoxenus, who uses a neutral third in both his *soft chromatic* tetrachords and his *hemiolic chromatic* tetrachords (fig. 14.13). However here he divides the remaining three dieses interval into two equal halves.

The point being made however, is that most of the various types of tetrachord obtained through what was in effect, a mathematical process of derivation, seem to be implicated. Is this a coincidence, or is it that the genera and shades are simply the fragments of what originally was a single enharmonic system? The answer may be the latter, because the enharmonic diesis is the only ground upon which all three of the genera ultimately settle. Therefore the difference between an intense and a soft shade comes down to a difference in magnitude of the upper interval of a tetrachord of one diesis. This is an enharmonic distinction, reflected by the audible difference between the shades. This distinction is only at home within the terms of the enharmonic genus.

Furthermore, the diatonic, chromatic and enharmonic genera are often discussed as if they were somehow mutually exclusive to one another, when in point of fact, the diatonic genus could not even exist without the fundamental ground provided for by the enharmonic genus. The proof of this is the obvious distinction between the major and the minor tone. In some modes of the diatonic scale the tone is major, while in others it is minor. The difference between the two is an enharmonic diesis, an interval that operates only at the enharmonic level.

The enharmonic diesis in this sense, is not a microtonal interval with a fixed magnitude. It is simply the indicator of the smallest differential of modal function, which in this example, finds its expression in the perceptible difference between the major tone of ratio 9/8 and the minor tone of 10/9. Consequently, the fundamental grounds for the scale system of ancient Greek music may indeed be enharmonic, and therefore perhaps most appropriately represented by an enharmonic scale of dieses.

Conclusion

Through our brief study of the musical scales belonging to the three genera, it is easy to see that the music of ancient Greece was distinguished by the use of a great variety of different scales and modes, these in total, representing the great treasures of the Greek scale system. Each genus clearly represents a complete world of modal colour and expression in its own right, the fundamental building block for which is the enharmonic diesis. In fact comparing this variety of modal expression that was available to Greek musicians, with modern Western equally tempered major and minor scales, shows how much Western music has actually lost.

Inevitably, some composers have attempted to reclaim some of this rich modal heritage. In terms of modern attempts, this includes the composers Harry Partch, in pieces such as *Windsong* and *Daphne of the Dunes* or indeed Lou Harrison in his extemporizations on ancient Greek modes in the 1970's. Although in its infancy, this process of the reclamation of vital features of what should be our musical heritage, will no doubt continue, and in the process of doing so, lead to the creation of some fascinating music.

Finney, author of a popular book on musical history once asked "Has Western music lost something by eliminating the melodic possibilities inherent in the smaller and less regular intervals which the music of other cultures still values".[70] Finney is referring here to the world of the enharmonic diesis, a world that in the West is still regarded as being something rather *esoteric*. This represents a very defensive attitude, especially in view of the fact that the music of virtually every other culture in the world, bar the West, has been treating such microtonal intervals as being perfectly normal and natural phenomenon of musical expression for thousands of years.

There again, while reconstructions of ancient Greek scales, as ideal models for the treatment of microtones in a melodic context, are indeed possible, there are certain features concerning the usage of those scales which will probably always remain a mystery. This is because, except for a few scarce fragments, nearly all of the ancient music has disappeared into time.

A part of the puzzle is undoubtedly the concept of *ethos,* which concerned itself with the effects of the music upon the human soul. All theorists and philosophers who discussed music made great mention of this quality. Aristides Quintilianus referred to the diatonic genus as being manly and austere, the chromatic as pathetic yet sweet while the enharmonic he considered animating and mild.[71]

These words are clearly referring to the perceived ethos of those scale systems. Greek philosophers had much to say on this

---

[70] Theodore M. Finney (1947), *A History of Music*, p. 9;

[71] Aristides Quintilianus, *On Music*, p. 111.

subject. Aristotle for example spoke on the ethos of particular modes describing the Mixolydian as being sad and grave; the Dorian as producing a moderate and settled temper and the Phrygian as inspiring enthusiasm.[72] Through the quality of modal ethos, it was therefore felt that music was capable of powerfully affecting the human disposition and character.

Clearly, a key part of that effect was the use and application of the particular modal ethos that a given situation required. Iamblichus (ca. 245-330) mentions this observing, "There are certain melodies devised as remedies against the passions of the soul, and also against despondency and lamentation, which Pythagoras invented as things that afford the greatest assistance in these maladies. Again, he employed other melodies against rage and anger, and against every aberration of the soul. There is also another kind of modulation invented as a remedy against desires".[73]

Note that Iamblichus refers to the effects of *melodies* upon the soul, rather than modes. This raises the question: how much was the ethos of a given mode due to the factors other than the scale used? Greek music was essentially an extemporized art and throughout the world, wherever extemporization is practiced on a systematic basis, clear frameworks for the process of extemporization are usually needed.

In Hindustani music, such frameworks are provided for by the *raga*, while in the near and Middle East, the *maqam* plays a similar role. In both cases, the scale or mode used is only one feature of this framework. Therefore, when the Greek modes

---

[72] Aristotle, *Politics*, 1340a.40.

[73] Iamblichus, *The Life of Pythagoras*, p. 62.

are studied, it is probable that each mode signified a framework for improvisation that itself, involved a synthesis of numerous elements, including that most abstract of qualities, the perceived ethos of the mode.

Again, looking at parallels with other bodies of modal music, Hindustani music has the concept of *rasa*, a series of nine archetypal emotions which music is capable of evoking in the listener. The performer, playing a certain raga, is consciously aware of the intended rasa, and everything in the performance is generally geared towards inculcating the required mind state in the listener. Indeed, the performer's skill is largely judged on the ability to do this. In this context, the performer is the living representative of a clearly established ancient tradition, a tradition which itself connects with a set of permanent and enduring values upon which the whole musical culture was generally founded.

There is no doubt that ancient Greek musicians were heir to such a musical tradition and that their skill and prowess as performers, was therefore judged accordingly. Although a part of that tradition, the body of scales used provides no more than a fragmentary picture of the tradition as a whole. A tradition about which only a rather sketchy picture has so far been obtained.

Index

acoustic science, 17
ajnas, 57
Al Farabi, 56-7
Al Kindi, 56
ancient Greek double octave, 35
ancient Greek tribes, 12, 74
Anne Kilmer, 79, 84, 86
apotome, 109, 141, 180, 182
Arabic maqamat, 56, 61
Arabic modal music, 56-7, 60-1, 112, 114, 191
Archytas, 7, 8, 13, 129, 157, 160, 161, 171-2, 199-200
Archytas diatonic scale, 7
Aristides Quintilianus, 111, 190, 204
Aristotle, 14, 19, 20, 45, 52, 54, 72, 94-5, 205, 218, 221
Aristoxenus, 4, 14-8, 37-9, 57, 107-18, 124-5, 149-57, 162-3, 170, 192, 199-201, 220
arithmetic, 18, 20, 43, 120, 127, 132
augmented fourth, 31, 79, 80-2, 103
authentic mode, 9
Babylonian harp, 85
..... music, 77, 79
..... tuning, 86
Baghdad Museum, 78
branch tetrachord, 60-1

C major scale, 54
Christian church, 8, 12, 77
Chroai, 106
chromatic genus, 136-7, 145-6 149, 153, 162, 174, 181
..... lichanós, 140, 145
..... octave species, 147
..... paranete, 141, 145
..... scale system, 140-2, 146, 150-1
..... system, 142-6, 150, 154-5, 160
chromatic tetrachord, 137-9, 141, 150, 151-7, 160-1, 200
church modes, 12
Cleonides, 72, 97
colours, 23, 61, 126, 136, 137, 186
comma of Didymus, 122
conjunct system, 66
..... tetrachords, 45, 55, 61, 63, 66, 101
consonance, 25, 28, 48
consonance and dissonance, 25
consonant intervals, 16, 49
consonant thirds and sixths, 84
Curt Sachs, 44, 142
cycle of fifths, 5, 67, 79, 180, 182-3
cyclic method of tuning, 80
dàn nguyêt lute, 175

Daniélou, 91, 189, 190
Daphne of the Dunes, 203
days of the week, 87-8
denominator, 27-31, 118, 120
Deuterus, 9, 10
devils fourth, 79
diapason, 26, 192
diapente, 26
diatessaron, 26
diatonic genus, 181, 196, 197
..... modes, 9, 12, 77, 82, 90, 97, 122
..... scale, 7, 8, 13, 70, 74, 77, 79, 80, 99, 113-14, 118, 120, 122, 126, 145, 178-80, 199, 201
..... semitone, 171
Didymus, 124, 161, 171, 200
Didymus' diatonic tuning, 124
diesis, 32, 129, 193, 199, 200-1
diezeugménon, 63-4, 68
Diodorus Siculus, 40-1
directions, 8, 23
disjunct tetrachords, 47, 63, 101
disjunctive tone, 99
dissonance, 28
ditonal diatonic shade, 118-19, 134
ditone, 16, 119, 120, 126-7, 152, 163, 172, 187
divisions of the monochord, 42
dominant, 10, 58, 59
Dorian, 10, 49, 50, 54-5, 60, 67, 70, 73-7, 90-101, 109, 112-13, 121-2, 129, 141-2, 151, 160, 163-4, 205

double octave, 34
dynamic mésē, 93-4
Earth, 24, 46, 87
Egypt, 40, 219
Egyptian temple, 40
eight medieval modes, 11
eight-note scale, 47
ekbole, 111, 190
eklysis,, 111, 190
elements, 2, 15, 19, 23, 40-1, 61, 105, 206
enharmonic diesis, 170, 182, 183, 191-6, 201-4
..... distinctions of tone, 186
..... genus, 137, 162-3, 171, 191, 201
..... pyknon, 163
..... scale, 39, 123, 130, 163-72, 182-94, 202
enharmonic scale of Olympus, 168
..... system, 164, 171-2, 193, 201
epimoric ratios, 118, 125, 129
epitritus ratio, 48
equable diatonic scale, 29-30, 133-4, 200
..... shade, 135
equal temperament, 5-8, 38, 40, 50, 106, 112, 123, 137, 188
Eratosthenes, 172
Euclid, 55, 221
even numbers, 20
faculties of the soul, 23
fine-tuning, 6-8, 13, 106-7, 124
first cause, 20
fixed tones, 47-9, 64, 92, 100,

102, 158, 183
four stages of creation, 22
four stringed lyre, 41
frequency relationship, 27
fundamental tone, 35
genera, 54, 137, 142-3, 162, 171-2, 181, 184, 192-203
genus, 54, 137-8, 142-5, 149-53, 163, 165, 171, 179, 184, 188-204
geometric figures, 23
Gioseffo Zarlino, 122
goddess of fertility, 84
greater perfect system, 54-5, 60-7, 72, 74-5, 90-2, 145
harmoniai, 73, 74, 75, 77, 93-4, 98, 111
harmonic major third, 30-1, 86, 187
..... minor third, 30, 31, 121
harmonic relationships, 28-9, 35, 86, 153
..... series, 35, 118, 133
harmony, 26, 40-1, 46, 49, 78, 84-5, 105, 120
harmony of the cosmos, 26
Harry Partch, 108, 203
Helmholtz, 133, 219
hemiolic chromatic shade, 150
heptachord, 44-7, 65, 83, 87-8
heptachord of Terpander, 44-7, 65, 83
Hermes, 41
Hindustani music, 205-6
Husayni makam, 133
hypátē, 51-5, 64, 73, 92, 99, 102, 110, 120, 125-7, 142, 145-6, 149, 151, 154, 160, 170, 189, 197
hýpaton tetrachord, 55, 64, 66
hyperbolaîon tetrachord, 63
Hypodorian, 74, 77, 92, 95, 100, 101, 147
Hypolydian, 74-5, 77, 94, 95, 99-103, 147
Hypophrygian, 74, 76, 77, 82, 92, 100-1, 147
Iamblichus, 205
immutable system, 68, 69
incomposite dieses, 111, 190
intense chromatic shade, 149, 153, 156
intense diatonic, 109-10, 113-4, 120-4, 130, 134, 155, 169, 193-4, 198-9
intervallic quality, 18, 19
Isartum, 85
Japan, 168
Japanese music, 5, 168, 198
jins, 57-60
Johann Kirnberger, 122
Joseph Campbell, 78
Jupiter, 46, 73
just tuning, 14
Kitab al-Adwar, 184
Kitab-al-Musiqa al-Kabir, 56
Lamprocles of Athens, 99
Leon Crickmore, 83, 88
lesser perfect system, 65-7
lichanós, 51, 53, 67, 110, 121, 124-5, 127, 138, 140-5, 149-54, 157, 160, 163, 166, 169,

170-1, 189, 196-8
Lou Harrison, 85, 203
lower tetrachord, 45, 48, 52, 60-1, 141
Lydian, 10, 74, 76, 77, 81, 90, 91, 94, 97, 98, 101, 122
lyre, 15, 33, 40-7, 51-4, 67, 78-80, 84, 91, 97, 101, 106, 143-4, 169, 192, 220
major and minor scale system, 11
major and minor scales, 4, 8, 203
major second, 112, 138
major semitone, 109
Malek Jandali, 85
maqam, 60, 205
Marcelle Duchesne-Guillemin, 79
Mars, 46, 73
mean-tone temperament, 14
Mercury, 46, 73
mésē, 33-4, 45-6, 51-5, 63, 65, 72-4, 92-7, 100-2, 110, 120-1, 126-7, 132, 138, 141-44, 149-52, 154, 157, 160, 163, 166, 196-8
méson tetrachord, 63-4, 145
Mesopotamia, 40, 219
minor mode, 61, 111, 140
..... second, 112, 120, 126
..... semitone, 109, 161
..... tone, 121-4, 126, 157, 160-1, 185, 187, 201-2
Mixolydian, 10, 74, 77, 92, 94, 95, 99, 101-3, 205

modal colour, 8, 106-7, 109, 203
..... dominant, 58-9
..... function, 71, 72, 202
..... system, 11, 136, 202-3
..... tonic, 10, 58-9, 70-3, 76, 119-20, 186
modulating scale systems, 67
modulation, 5, 90, 97, 205
monochord, 32, 34, 35
movable notes, 47-8, 107, 136
movable tones, 47, 49
music of the spheres, 46, 78
musical experience, 14-9, 38-9
musical intervals, 16, 18, 25, 28, 35, 107, 118
musical scale, 13-4, 16, 20, 24, 29, 40-4, 64, 70, 73, 105, 178
natural acoustic principles, 36
nétē, 51-2, 55, 64-5, 92, 141, 143, 146
neutral second, 112, 116, 193
..... seventh, 116
..... sixth, 116, 151
..... third, 116, 150, 193, 199, 201
..... tone, 112, 125, 151, 154, 160, 189, 191-2, 200
Nicomachus, 24, 41, 44, 45, 47, 73, 87
Nid Qablim, 81, 82
Nis Gabari, 80
non-modulating scale systems, 67
note ratios, 16, 25, 29, 38, 108, 117, 153
numbers, 10, 19, 20-31, 34-6,

41-3, 64, 86, 89, 92, 120-1, 132, 134, 155-8, 193-4
numbers of the decade, 20, 22, 121
numerator, 27, 28, 30, 31, 118
octave, 5-6, 15-6, 19, 25-6, 29, 32-4, 37, 39, 42-3, 47, 48, 50-1, 53, 55, 59-64, 70-1, 74-6, 82, 86, 88, 90-3, 95, 99, 106, 108-9, 114, 118, 122-3, 130, 133, 145-6, 151, 153, 164-5, 177, 185, 187, 194
octave circle, 6, 34
octoechos, 9
odd and even numbers, 10, 20
Olympus, 166, 168, 169, 188, 189
On Osiris and Isis, 40
Paramésē, 52, 73
Paranétē, 52, 73
Parhypátē, 52, 53, 73, 121
pentachord, 57
pentatonic, 5, 44, 142-7, 165-6, 168, 175, 178, 183, 196-8
perfect consonances, 48
Phrygian, 7, 10, 74, 77, 95, 96, 97, 98, 101, 122, 205
pitch, 16, 19, 25, 32-4, 44-5, 51, 55-6, 90-1, 95, 106, 125, 127, 137-8, 149, 153, 163, 188
pitch continuum, 32-3
Pitum, 82
plagal mode, 9-10
planetary harmonies, 87
Plato, 20-1, 54, 94-5
Plato's Lambda, 176

Plutarch, 40, 44-5, 49, 97, 99, 143, 162-3, 166, 168, 189, 192-3, 199, 201
Pope Gregory, 9
Porphyry, 108, 221
primary forces of the cosmic order, 23
prime number, 86, 125, 134, 158
proslambanómenos, 55-6, 63, 67
Protus, 9, 10
Ptolemy, 29-30, 57, 90, 92, 95, 117-18, 120-35, 153-61, 169-70, 199-200
pyknon, 149, 151-7, 161, 163, 169, 17-2
Pythagoras, 19, 24-6, 32, 38-40, 43, 47, 86, 107, 117, 205, 221
Pythagorean comma, 108, 181, 182
Pythagorean cyclic method of scale division, 176
..... philosophy, 20
..... teachings, 19, 21
..... Tetractys, 21-2, 24, 64
..... tuning, 13-4, 50, 53, 79, 86, 103, 106, 109, 118-20, 134, 141, 150, 172, 200
Pythagoreans, 19, 20, 22, 23, 24, 26, 37, 38, 117
quartertone, 39, 107, 111, 114, 116, 165, 169-72
raga, 205-6
Rast maqam, 112
ratio, 25-31, 34-8, 43, 48-9, 59,

64, 80, 86, 102-3, 108-9, 118, 119-26, 130, 132, 134, 141, 154, 157, 161, 169, 171-2, 177, 180-1, 185, 194, 199, 202
Richard Dumbrill, 86
root and branch tetrachords, 60-1
Royal Tomb of Ur, 78
Safi al Din, 184, 186
Safi al-Din al-Urmawi, 184
Sarcadas of Argos, 97
Saturn, 46, 73, 87
Scott Marcus, 57, 60
seasons, 23, 41
Sections of a Canon, 55
semitone, 6, 16, 30, 31-2, 44-5, 51, 76, 81, 96, 100, 107-9, 110, 113, 121, 126-7, 137-8, 141-2, 145-6, 149-50, 152, 154, 157, 160-4, 169, 171-2, 178-95, 197, 199
septimal harmony, 36
Serenade for Guitar and Percussion, 85
seven chromatic modes, 148
..... enharmonic modes, 167
..... heavens, 46
..... heptatonic modes, 82
..... modes, 77, 79, 90, 92, 95, 101-3, 113-4, 123, 126, 130, 133, 146, 158, 165
..... octave species, 75
..... planets, 46, 87
sevenfold cosmological scheme, 47
seventh harmonic, 36, 126

shades, 57, 105-7, 109-10, 114, 117-20, 131, 134-7, 150, 153, 157, 160, 181, 194-5, 199, 201
slack Lydian, 94
soft chromatic shade, 152-3, 157
soft chromatic tetrachord, 152, 158
soft diatonic, 109, 110, 111, 112, 113, 114, 124, 125, 126, 134, 138, 154, 161, 198, 200
song of the moon-bull, 78
sphere of the sun, 47, 73
spiral of fifths, 181, 187-8
spondaeiasmos, 111, 190
Spondeion mode, 168, 189
St Ambrose, 9
Stefan Hagel, 52, 54
symphonies, 25
synēmménōn tetrachord, 65
Terpander of Lesbos, 44-6
Tetractys, 21-5, 32, 34, 41, 64, 86, 92, 118, 120
tetrad, 23, 25
tetrahedron, 23
Tetrardus, 9
The Elements of Harmony., 14
Theodosius Macrobius, 41
thetic and dynamic mésē, 92-4
three main diatonic modes, 97
three perfect consonances, 25, 43
three-dimensional world, 23
Tomb of Ur, 78
tonal centers, 91
tone of disjunction, 47, 48, 56,

61, 63, 98-101, 113, 151, 154, 163, 170
tonos, 90-3
trichord, 145, 196, 197
trihemitone, 119, 138, 141, 146, 150, 154, 177, 199
trítē, 52
Tritus, 9
tuning, 5-8, 13-5, 40-4, 50, 52, 57, 67, 79, 80-1, 84-5, 88, 101-2, 106, 109, 114, 118, 122-4, 130-3, 140, 143, 150, 153, 157-8, 160-1, 168-9, 171, 172
twelve unique divisions of the tetrachord, 195
two octave expression of maqam, 60

Ugarit, 79, 84, 85, 87, 219, 220
unity, 20, 23, 28, 29, 34, 35, 118, 120, 134
Venus, 46, 73
vibration numbers, 27
Vietnam, 175
vong cô mode, 175
whole tone, 15, 16, 25-6, 31-2, 49, 75, 76, 108-9, 112-13, 118-9, 126-7, 129-30, 132, 141, 146, 164, 177, 181, 186, 191, 197-9
whole tone diatonic tetrachord, 127-9
Windsong, 203
yin and yang, 20
ziggurat of Borsippa, 87

Bibliography

Barker, A. (2004). *Greek Musical Writings: Harmonic and Acoustic Theory.* London: Cambridge University Press.

Barker, A. (1984). *Greek Musical Writings: The Musician and his Art.* Cambridge: Cambridge University Press.

Barry, P. (Vol. 5, No. 4 (Oct 1919)). Greek Music. *The Music Quarterly* , 578 - 613.

Becker, J. (1969). Anatomy of a Mode. *Ethnomusicology, Vol. 13, No. 2* , 267 - 279.

Butcher, S. H. (2010). *The Poetics of Aristotle.* Createspace.

Campbell, J. (1993). *The Hero with a Thousand Faces.* London: Fontana Press.

Campbell, J. (2008). *The Mythic Dimension: Selected Essays 1959 - 1987.* Novato: New World Library.

Chalmers, J. (1990). *Divisions of the Tetrachord.* Lebanon: Frog Peak Music.

Christensen, T. S. (2002). *The Cambridge History of Western Music Theory.* Cambridge: Cambridge University Press.

Crickmore, L. (2008). New Light on the Babylonian Tonal System. *ICONEA* , 11 - 22.

Crickmore, L. (2013, April 28). *Planets, Heptachords and the Days of the Week - the Harmony of the Spheres.* Retrieved from Academia.edu: www.academia.edu

Danielou, A. (1979). *Introduction to the Study of Musical Scales.* Columbia: South Asia Books.

Danielou, A. (1968). *Northern Indian Music.* New York: Frederick A.

Praeger.

Danielou, A. (1968). *The Ragas of Northern Indian Music.* London: Barrie & Jenkins.

Datta, P. (2009). *Understanding Indian Classical Music.* Archive of North Indian Classical Music .

Duchesne-Guillemin, M. (1984). A Hurrian Musical Score from Ugarit: The Discovery of Mesopotamian Music. *Sources from the Ancient Near East, Vol. 2 Fascicle 2* , 5 - 26.

Duchesne-Guillemin, M. (1981). Music in Ancient Mesopotamia and Egypt. *World Archeology, Vol. 12. No. 3. Feb.* , 287-297.

Dumbrill, R. (2005). *The Archemomusicology of the Ancient Near East.* London: Trafford Publishing.

Ellis, A. (1885). On the Musical Scales of Various Nations. *Journal of the Society of Arts, No. 33* .

Evans, J. A. (2005). *Arts and Humanities Through the Eras: Ancient Greece and Rome (1200 B.C.E. - 476 C.E.).* Farmington Hill: Thompson-Gale.

Ficino, M. (n.d.). *On Divine Frenzy (De divino furore).* Retrieved from http://www-rohan.sdsu.edu/~lavoicy/labe/ficino-frenzy.htm

Finney, T. M. (1947). *A History of Music, Rev. Ed.* . New York: Harcourt.

Godwin, J. (1993). *The Harmony of the Spheres.* Rochester: Inner Traditions.

Godwin, J. (1991). *The Mystery of the Seven Vowels in Theory and Practise.* Grand Rapids: Phanes Press.

Harrison, L. (1971). The Tuning of the Babylonian Harp, KPFA.

Hegel, S. (2010). *Ancient Greek Music: A Technical History.* Cambridge: Cambridge University Press.

Helmholtz, H. (1954). *On the Sensations of Tone.* New York: Dover

Publications.

Hewitt, M. (2013). *Musical Scales of the World.* Note Tree Press.

Herodotus. (2009). *The History of Herodotus: Translated from the Ancient Greek by George Rawlinson (V. 1) (1909).* Cornell: Cornell University Library.

Ingram, R. W. (Vol 26, Issue 3 - 4, June 1932). Aristoxenus and the Intervals of Greek Music. *The Classical Quarterly* , p. 195 - 208.

Jandali, M. (Composer). (2009). *Echoes from Ugarit* (Album). [M. Jandali, Performer]

Kemp, J. (Vol. 13, No. 2, Oct 1966). Professional Musicians in Ancient Greece. *Greece and Rome,* 213 - 222.

Lyre of Ur. (2011). Retrieved June 16th, 2011, from http://www.lyre-of-ur.com/history.htm

Marcus, S. L. (1989). *Arab Music Theory in the Modern Period.* Michigan: U.M.I.

Mathiesen, T. J. (1999). *Apollo's Lyre - Greek Music and Music Theory in Antiquity and the Middle Ages.* Lincoln and London: University of Nebraska Press.

Mountford, J. F. (Vol. 40, Part 1 (1920)). Greek Music and its Relation to Modern Times. *The Journal of Hellenic Studies* , 13 - 42.

Munro, D. B. (1894). *The Modes of Ancient Greek Music.* Oxford: Clarendon Press.

Nguyen, Phong Th., Restructuring the Fixed Pitches of the Vietnamese Dan Nguyet Lute: A Modification Necessitated by the Modal system. *Asian Music,* Vol. 18, no. 1, Autumn-Winter, p. 56 – 70.

Ovid. (2009). *Metamorphoses (Oxford World's Classics) trans. by A. D. Meliville.* Oxford: Oxford University Press .

Palisca, C. V. (vol. 3, no. 3 (Summer 1984)). Introductory Notes on the

Historiography of the Greek Modes. *The Journal of Musicology*, 221 - 228.

Partch, H. (1974). *Genesis of a Music.* New York: Da Capo Press.

Porphyry. (1920). *The Life of Pythagoras translated by Kenneth Guthrie*.

Powers, C. (2006). *Arabic Musical Scales: Basic Maqam Notation.* Boulder, U.S.A: G.L. Design.

Proclus. (1992). *A Commentary on the First Book of Euclid's Elements, trans. by Glen Morrow.* Princeton: Princeton University Press.

Ross, W. D. (2012). *The Metaphysics by Aristotle Ed. by Roger Bishop Jones, trans. by W. D. Ross.* London: Createspace.

S.H.Butcher. (1997). *Aristotle: Poetics.* New York: Dover Publications.

Sachs, C. (2008). *The Rise of Music in the Ancient World.* London: Dover Publications.

Sachs, C. (1962). *The Wellsprings of Music.* The Hague: Martinus Nijhoff.

Savas, J. (1975). *Byzantine Music: Theory and Practice.* Boston: Holy Cross Orthodox Press.

Shirlaw, M. (Vol. 32, No. 2 (Apr. 1951)). The Music and Tone Systems of Ancient Greece. *Music and Letters*, 131 - 139.

Strunk, O. (1950). *Source Readings in Music History.* New York: W. W. Norton and Company, Inc.

The Oldest Song in the World. (2006). Retrieved from Amaranth Publishing: http://www.amaranthpublishing.com/hurrian.htm

Williams, C. A. (1898). The Notes Mese and Hypate in Greek Music. *The Classical Review*, 98 - 100.

Winnington-Ingram, R. P. (Dec. 1956). The Pentatonic Tuning of the Greek Lyre. *Classical Quarterly, Vol. 6, Issue 3 - 4*, 169 - 186.

Winnington-Ingram, R. P. (Apr. 1928). The Spondeion Scale. *The Classical Quarterly, Vol. 22, No. 2* , 83 - 91.

About the Author

Dr Mike Hewitt is a composer, author and lecturer currently living in North Wales. He earned a bachelor of music degree from the University of London and a master of music degree and doctorate from the University of North Wales, Bangor. He is author of numerous books on music, including the popular series of books for computer musicians. These include *Music Theory for Computer Musicians; Composition for Computer Musicians* and *Harmony for Computer Musicians*.

www.ingramcontent.com/pod-product-compliance
Lightning Source LLC
Chambersburg PA
CBHW070737160426
43192CB00009B/1474